ALSO BY LINDA SCHIERSE LEONARD

The Wounded Woman: Healing the Father-Daughter Relationship

On the Way to the Wedding: Transforming the Love Relationship

Witness to the Fire: Creativity and the Veil of Addiction

Meeting the Madwoman: Empowering the Feminine Spirit

CREATION'S

HEARTBEAT

Following the Reindeer Spirit

LINDA SCHIERSE LEONARD, PH.D.

BANTAM BOOKS

NEW YORK·TORONTO·LONDON·SYDNEY·AUCKLAND

CREATION'S HEARTBEAT

A Bantam Book / December 1995

Books and articles quoted or cited in the text under the usual fair allowances are acknowledged in the notes. The author is grateful for permission to use more extensive quotations from the following sources: *Collected Poems* by W. H. Auden, edited by Edward Mendelson. Copyright © by W. H. Auden. Reprinted by permission of Random House, Inc.; *Letters of Rainer Maria Rilke 1910–1926,* translated from the German by Jane Bannard Greene and M. D. Herter Norton, with the permission of W. W. Norton & Company, Inc. Copyright © 1947, 1948 by W. W. Norton & Company, Inc., renewed © 1975 by M. D. Herter Norton; *Duino Elegies* by Rainer Maria Rilke, translated from the German by J. B. Leishman and Stephen Spender, with the permission of W. W. Norton & Company, Inc. Copyright © 1939 by W. W. Norton & Company, Inc., renewed © by J. B. Leishman and Stephen Spender; *Letters to a Young Poet* by Rainer Maria Rilke, translated from the German by M. D. Herter Norton, with the permission of W. W. Norton & Company, Inc. Copyright © 1934, 1954 by W. W. Norton & Company, Inc., renewed © 1962, 1982 by M. D. Herter Norton; *The Man Who Killed the Deer* by Frank Waters, reprinted with the permission of the Ohio University Press/Swallow Press, Athens, Ohio; *An Interrupted Life: The Diaries of Etty Hillesum, 1941–1943,* by Etty Hillesum, ed. J. G. Gaarlandt, with the permission of Random House, Inc., Copyright © 1981 by De Haan/Uniebock b.v., Bussum, English translation copyright by Jonathon Cape, Ltd., 1983; Permission granted by Karl Kopp to reprint part of his poem, "Deer" from his book, *Yarbrough Mountain,* published by Baleen Press, 1977, Phoenix, AZ.; Permission granted by Mary Elizabeth Williams to print her poems: "The Fan Maker" and "How the Old Woman Met Death."

Book design by Jessica Shatan
Map design by GDS / Jeffrey L. Ward

Library of Congress Cataloging-in-Publication Data
Leonard, Linda Schierse.
   Creation's heartbeat : following the reindeer spirit / Linda Schierse Leonard.
      p.   cm.
   Includes bibliographical references and index.
   ISBN 0-553-07300-1
   1. Arctic regions—Religion. 2. Arctic regions—Description and travel.
3. Reindeer—Religious aspects. 4. Shamanism—Arctic regions. 5. Feminism—
Religious aspects. 6. Women and religion. 7. Leonard, Linda Schierse.
I. Title.
BL2670.L46   1995
299'.4—dc20   95-9141   CIP

Published simultaneously in the United States and Canada

Bantam Books are published by Bantam Books, a division of Bantam Doubleday Dell Publishing Group, Inc. Its trademark, consisting of the words "Bantam Books" and the portrayal of a rooster, is Registered in U.S. Patent and Trademark Office and in other countries. Marca Registrada. Bantam Books, 1540 Broadway, New York, New York 10036.

PRINTED IN THE UNITED STATES OF AMERICA
BVG   10 9 8 7 6 5 4 3 2 1

Contents

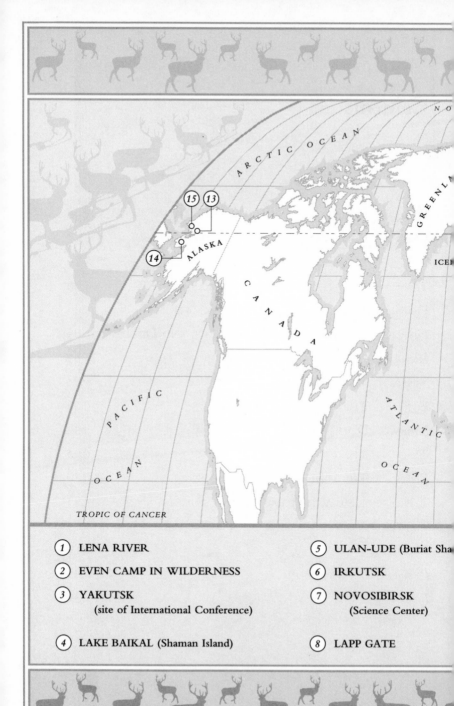

1. LENA RIVER

2. EVEN CAMP IN WILDERNESS

3. YAKUTSK
   (site of International Conference)

4. LAKE BAIKAL (Shaman Island)

5. ULAN-UDE (Buriat Sha...

6. IRKUTSK

7. NOVOSIBIRSK
   (Science Center)

8. LAPP GATE

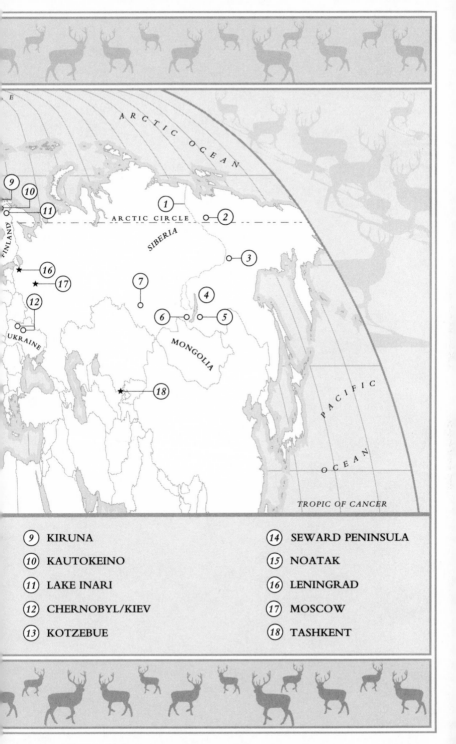

ARCTIC OCEAN

ARCTIC CIRCLE

SIBERIA

FINLAND

UKRAINE

MONGOLIA

PACIFIC

OCEAN

TROPIC OF CANCER

⑨ KIRUNA

⑩ KAUTOKEINO

⑪ LAKE INARI

⑫ CHERNOBYL/KIEV

⑬ KOTZEBUE

⑭ SEWARD PENINSULA

⑮ NOATAK

⑯ LENINGRAD

⑰ MOSCOW

⑱ TASHKENT

Prologue

DREAM OF THE
REINDEER WOMAN

About ten years ago, my soul mate, Keith, woke me at dawn to tell me the following dream.

I was in a cold white room with other physicians and their wives. Immediately I felt alienated. All of the people at this gathering were formal, stiff, and staid and were dressed as though they wanted to show off their wealth and prestige. Everywhere I turned I heard only small talk and these professionals' attempts to impress one another with their importance. I was uncomfortable, and I looked around to find something genuine or a way to escape. I saw a white piano in the room and walked toward it, wanting to sit down and play. But when I tried to play the piano, the atmosphere was so cold that I couldn't create. I felt a lack of soul in the room, and I knew I had to leave.

I suddenly saw an exit at the back of the room and walked rapidly toward it. When I crossed the threshold, I entered into an amazing space. All of the doors and windows of this new room opened out onto a vast wilderness. I was astonished to see a woman, her hair blown by the wind, suddenly run into the room from the forest. She wore deerskin clothing. In amazement I asked: "Who are you, and where have you been?" She answered: "I've just returned from a journey. I have run for months with a herd of pregnant reindeer." I awoke feeling: "This is what I want also—to run with the pregnant reindeer."

I found this image of the woman who ran with the reindeer wonderfully inspiring. Keith and I often ran together in nature—through ancient redwood forests, along high cliffs above the sea, over mountain ridges and down through grassy valleys, and by sand dunes near the ocean's edge. During these runs we sometimes encountered deer and marveled at their fleetness of foot, their beauty and grace. And we imagined we were deer as we ran with their spirit before us. I recognized the Reindeer Woman's energy as the kind I experience when I feel the brisk wind on my skin, breathe the fresh air, smell the forest fragrance, and touch the soft pine needles under my feet in the woods and on mountain trails. Running with the pregnant reindeer is a compelling image of the feminine embodiment of creative spirit, the same spirit I sense when I am hiking in nature.

Thousands of pregnant reindeer moving through the wilderness to give birth, the image of the self-sufficient herd itself, strikes me as a vivid symbol of women's archetypal generative journey with their sisters. I learned that reindeer do make an actual migration every spring and travel hundreds of miles north from April to June to bear their young, enduring the harshest conditions of the Arctic wilderness, a journey that speaks to feminine endurance and power, the will to survive. Female reindeer also have antlers with which they can protect themselves and their newborn. Deer are not predators, and indeed, for many cultures they embody the power of the heart. To me, the Reindeer Woman image expresses a free-spirited, wild, and strong femininity that is also gentle and compassionate.

Intuitively, I felt that the Reindeer Woman could become a healing metaphor for others, as well. Because this living symbol of instinctual feminine energy evokes kind-hearted, mystical, and creative qualities, I felt it could inspire women and men alike in their spiritual development. This image drew me back to the end of my first book, *The Wounded Woman: Healing the Father-Daughter Relationship,* where I concluded that finding and integrating feminine spirit is a central task for women and men today and is a prerequisite to living a spiritual, ecological, and peaceful way of life. But, because I was in the midst of writing another book, I felt I had to allow the image of the Reindeer Woman to germinate in my psyche. I sensed I would return to her, learn more about her, and honor her mysterious presence when I was ready.

At the time of Keith's dream, I was writing my third book, *Witness to the Fire: Creativity and the Veil of Addiction.* The process of writing that book—and the process I was writing about—emphasized for me that vulnerability and receptivity are essential to creativity and that addictions destroy these

qualities. In particular, by denigrating gentleness and vulnerability and by confusing these qualities with victimization,
addictions to control and power endanger the entire world.

In the spring of 1986, shortly after Keith's dream of the
Reindeer Woman, we traveled to Russia. For years we had
immersed ourselves in Russian literature, history, music, bal-
let, opera, poetry, and film, and we felt close to the Russian
soul. I especially wanted to visit the home of Dostoyevsky
because his life and writing had influenced my own spiritual
path, had illuminated the interior psychological forces inherent in addiction and creativity, and also had shown me a way
to spiritual transformation.

First we went to Moscow to see where Dostoyevsky was
born and raised. From Moscow we traveled to Tashkent in
south-central Asia, near the border of Afghanistan—the area
of the ancient silk route and the place where political dissi-
dents, like the poet Anna Akhmatova, were exiled during the
Communist era. Without explanation, we were detained in
Tashkent for several days by Soviet authorities. We felt frus-
trated and angry at this confinement, but we had no choice
in the matter.

When we were allowed to proceed, we traveled to Leningrad where we visited Dostoyevsky's home and the
Haymarket area, which is the setting for his novel, *Crime and
Punishment*. On a day when Russians celebrate an Easter
ceremony, we visited his graveside in the Alexandr Nevsky
Monastery cemetery, where many great artists and scientists
are buried. As we participated in the Easter services and
procession, we saw the wisened faces of old women, the
grandmothers, or babushkas as they are called in Russia,
kneeling to pray before the icons of the holy mother. We
smelled the fragrant scent of incense and burning candles,

heard the chanting of the monks and worshipers and the reverberations of the ringing bells, and knew that spirituality was still alive in many Russian people's hearts. I cried at Dostoyevsky's graveside, where a great statue in his honor was covered with flowers, which people brought daily to pay homage to him.

We felt the conflict between Dostoyevsky's gentle, mystical teachings and the cold, rational dogma reflected in the stony faces of Soviet patriarchs that loomed from huge posters hung high on monolithic city buildings. As we walked along the misty Neva river in Leningrad, we began to feel something in the air, as though an ominous threat was drifting out of the dark clouds, stifling us and many of the Russian people, too. Only at the airport in Leningrad, just before we boarded the plane to return home, did we learn that our delay in Tashkent had been due to the Chernobyl nuclear disaster and that winds had scattered the fallout to Leningrad and northward toward the Arctic Circle.

At first we were shocked, appalled, and angry at the Soviet authorities for denying, then covering up this calamity. Then, as the rumors gradually coalesced into the horrifying facts of this man-made catastrophe, we felt despair that human beings were destroying each other. A Kafkaesque mood of disbelief, dread, and helplessness descended upon us. On our way from Moscow to Tashkent and back to Leningrad, we had actually flown through the nuclear clouds of Chernobyl without knowing it. This was a direct collision with the atomic clouds of the World's Dark Night, the global Dark Night of the Soul resulting from addiction to power— the very issue about which I was writing in *Witness to the Fire*.

Chernobyl's fallout, we learned, had adversely affected the health of the reindeer—not to mention the health of the serene people who follow them. This convergence of worldly experience and dream image reinforced my growing view of the reindeer as a totemic animal for the peaceful, creative, gentle spirit of the heart. Indeed, the endangerment of the reindeer reflects our own human predicament within the global environmental crisis.

The native peoples of the Far North who follow the reindeer revere these wild and gentle creatures as sacred. Later, as I was gradually drawn to follow the image of the reindeer and research this book, I returned to Russia to sojourn with the Even people in Siberia and with other peoples of the Arctic. My experience with these peoples taught me that reindeer embody qualities of endurance and survival, and that they can symbolize these potential strengths in our own human lives. The reindeer's ability to adapt to the demands of nature, particularly their arduous annual spring migration to their northern birthing grounds, became for me an apt reminder of our human cultural need to value and embody the wild, indomitable feminine spirit as well as our need to follow Nature's rhythms and to uncover a path for peace.

One

FOLLOWING A
DREAM

he dream of the Reindeer Woman called to me so insistently that I took several years' leave of absence from my established profession as a therapist in order to answer it. I did not know where the dream journey might lead me, nor why I was making such a sacrifice. Over the next four years, it led me to the Siberian wilderness to live with nomadic reindeer people, to Lapland to learn about the Sami culture, and to Alaska to search for migrating caribou. Inwardly, I entered upon a spiritual quest that challenged me to look at myself and my life anew.

I have always been a journeyer, as all of us—in the great archetypal sense—are. At birth we make the great journey from our mother's womb, and at death we make the final passage. In my own childhood, I had escaped the trauma of my unhappy family life by traveling with imaginary friends to distant lands. I joined the heroines and heroes of my favorite books and fairy tales and shared their adventures and quests to find a better world, one with a meaning that transcended the pain and superficiality of shallow existence.

Later, as an adult, I studied the paths of poets, novelists, and philosophers, feeling a kinship with them in their desire to understand the purpose of life and to envision a better way of living. Through the autobiographies of creative people, I explored how they expressed their personal and universal truths. As a teacher of philosophy, I shared these quests with my students; as a Jungian analyst, I listened to the stories and worked with the unfolding dreams of people who had embarked on an inner search for healthier, more creative, and more spiritual lives.

My own inner journey—some thirty years of recording and learning from my dreams and visions—has been seasoned by my outer travels in faraway lands. I have trekked through jungles and ridden elephants in Thailand, climbed Mount Kilimanjaro in Africa, explored the art and temples of India and Nepal, crossed deserts by camel, boated down the Nile and the Amazon, hiked over high passes from country to country in the Alps, and backpacked through the windy wilderness of Tasmania and of Patagonia. But it was when I traveled to the Arctic that I truly followed a dream.

Indigenous peoples all over the world honor dreams and the wisdom they contain. Native people are aware that the dream of one person in the tribe can have meaning for the whole community. Such a dream may reveal an issue or value that the entire community has neglected and that they need to understand and integrate into their lives. Keith's dream of the Reindeer Woman struck me as this kind of "big dream," one that comes from the shared blueprint of the soul that Jung called the collective unconscious, and that speaks to us across time and cultural divisions to reveal important universal human truths.

After I finished writing *Witness to the Fire* in spring 1989, I was driving with Keith over Independence Pass in the Rocky Mountains, an alpine area at an altitude where the land resembles the Arctic tundra. Suddenly, coming over the car radio, we heard *Finlandia,* Sibelius's symphonic poem. Through the music and the mountains, we felt the soul of the North. To my own surprise, I heard myself say, "*Finlandia!* Let's go to the Arctic where the reindeer run." Keith readily agreed since we were both so moved by his dream. So we decided to explore its significance, both in the physical world and in the realm of the psyche.

Eventually, the dream led us to make three trips to the Arctic—to Lapland, Alaska, and the wilds of Siberia—in our quest to encounter reindeer. We met with the Sami and Even peoples, who follow the reindeer. We wanted to look into the eyes of these mysterious creatures and the people who revered them. When we saw them roaming freely in their natural habitat, the Arctic, we sensed how dream and reality are part of the one great life that is whole.

Early in the autumn of 1989, Keith and I took our first trip to the land of the reindeer, the far northern area of the Arctic Circle—a vast stretch of land that covers Sweden, Norway, Finland, and Russia. There one feels overwhelmed by space. Boundaries seem to disappear. Horizons and landscapes shift their shape. The outlines of humans and animals alike, of plants and stones, of trees and mountains, disappear in the mist. Roads and markers appear to vanish. Light bewitches

and beckons one to unearthly realms beyond ordinary consciousness. This is the land of the midnight sun where, for
the greater part of the year, things dissolve in uncanny white-
ness.

Time, too, is altered in the North and itself alters ordinary
perceptions. For several winter months the sun disappears.
Reindeer and the people who follow them live through the
Arctic winter's seemingly interminable dark days and then
readjust to the continuous white nights of sunlit summers.
The northern sense of time contrasts with the more linear
perception in temperate climes. The North is mystical—it
encompasses the snow, the shimmering light, the twilight
zone that we all experience at the borders of the conscious
and the unconscious. There both darkness and light are part
of a greater whole.

The reindeer are mysterious; they challenge our imagination. Reindeer know their way through the vast Arctic night.
When Keith and I first wandered around the immense tundra
of Lapland in search of the elusive reindeer, I began to see
them as symbolically related to the mystics who explore the
Dark Night of the Soul. Like spiritual questers who, when
lost in the soul's wilderness, find their path anew, the reindeer move through the ever-shifting winter snowdrifts that
suggest the "clouds of unknowing" described by mystics.
They are the animal spirits that symbolize the mystical life.
Both the mystic and the reindeer dwell in a great emptiness, a
realm of sacred space.

We were very naive on this first trip, thinking we could
quickly discover the nature of reindeer. We actually began
our journey in France, where Paleolithic images of reindeer
were discovered in the Lascaux caves. From there we traveled
north by train to Kiruna, a city in the Swedish part of Lap-

land. I think we expected to see reindeer the minute we stepped from the train, but day after day, as we drove around in our rented car, none were in evidence.

Finally, a bit embarrassed by our ignorance, we asked where they were. We were told, "Head for the mountains. They are probably there, in the middle of their migration, ready to return to their autumn home. Sometimes they are all over Kiruna, and you can hardly cross the street without bumping into them, but now you will have to wander around until you find them."

As we drove toward the mountains, we reached a pass on the border of Sweden and Norway. The winds were raging, but the storm lifted briefly to show the most brilliant, multicolored, glowing rainbow we had ever seen. The rainbow seemed to be a gift and a sign that finally we would find the elusive reindeer spirit. A border guard told us that the pass was always strangely stormy, even when the weather was clear on either side. This was the location of the legendary Lapp Gate.

For the Sami people, the indigenous inhabitants of Lapland, the Lapp Gate is a passageway to the other world, the gateway through which the mystical reindeer, the spirit animal of the ancient shamans, leaps in flight into the transcendental realm. The Lapp Gate is a "cosmic center," a meeting place between the finite and infinite realms. It is the threshold between two worlds—between consciousness and unconsciousness, earth and heaven, matter and spirit, death and rebirth, the beginning and ending of mortal life. It is the bridge between spirit and nature.

Seeing the rainbow and feeling the presence of the Lapp Gate and the reindeer spirit, we continued, driving to the west coast of Norway, then up and around the jagged coast line. As we were beginning to feel again that we were on a fool's chase, we came upon a sign that said "Kautokeino." On a hunch, we headed south through a deep, winding gorge with strange stone formations. There in the quiet solitude of the rugged ochre chasm, we felt the kind of awe evoked by the power of a sacred site. "Soon," Keith said, "we'll see our first reindeer."

Within the hour, we spotted them, half-hidden in the birch woods where they were grazing. We gazed at them in wonder for so long that we lost all sense of time. Ranging in color from brown to white, they blended into the birch trees like forest spirits, their antlers like moving birch branches. From a distance, the pure white reindeer resembled unicorns, and we understood why it had once been forbidden to kill them: They were believed to carry the souls of humans who had died and passed to the other world.

As we traveled through Norway and into Finland, we encountered more and more reindeer. In Finland, hiking over the high rocky, rounded fells, we saw them gliding through the mist, appearing and disappearing like apparitions. I wanted to run with them in my imagination, to follow their flight toward the ineffable secret they seemed to hold.

We also learned about the Sami people who follow them and honor their infallible instincts. This was not easy since many of these beautiful, gentle people seemed to have forgotten their sacred stories and the healing practices of their ancestors. As a nomadic people, the ancient Samis were guided by their shamans and by their beliefs in natural powers and in the healing powers of the shaman's drum. Several centuries ago, however, Christian patriarchs took away the Samis' ritual drums and forbade them to worship at their traditional sacred sites. On this first trip to find the reindeer, I gathered as many myths and stories as I could, talked to local anthropologists, and asked the native people, including a reindeer herdress and her mother, about their own reindeer dreams. Yet in the few weeks I was there, I realized that I had much more to learn and that I would have to return to reindeer country soon.

Back in the United States, I continued to investigate the mysterious significance of the reindeer by researching their actual habits and physiognomy and by collecting myths and stories about them. I discovered that many women and men were also having powerful reindeer dreams, while others were writing reindeer poems. Women artists were painting antlered deer and self-portraits with antlers on their heads. Reindeer obviously had a universal, cross-cultural significance and meaning.

Two summers later, in 1991, Keith and I returned to the Arctic Circle—this time to Alaska, to seek out the caribou, the American relatives of the reindeer indigenous to Europe and Asia. We wanted to see the caribou migration if we could, and I wanted to find out if the native peoples in Alaska had the same nomadic ways and the same practical and mythic relationship with caribou as the Sami people have with reindeer. In the early part of this century, a herd of reindeer were brought to Alaska by some Sami people to help the Eskimos learn animal husbandry, so perhaps they shared attitudes and practices, since reindeer and caribou share certain characteristics. For instance, both reindeer and caribou live in the Arctic, travel hundreds of miles every year to give birth, and have antlered females.

From Kotzebue, an Inuit town above the Arctic Circle, we flew with a bush pilot over the Noatak National Preserve, where forest rangers had spotted a moving herd a day earlier.

However, we were unable to find any caribou that day. We continued on to the Seward Peninsula where we were told we might see both caribou and reindeer. But after we arrived in Nome, we learned that the antlers of reindeer there had been severed because, in their velvet stage, they can be made into aphrodisiacs and sold for great profit in Asia. Horrified by this discovery, we sought solace in nature. While hiking, we saw in the distance a lone reindeer swimming across a river, and Keith also spotted some reindeer antlers that lay hidden in a rocky crevice. We assumed that this set of antlers had been shed by "the reindeer who got away" and treasured it as a gift from our totemic animal to encourage us on our journey.

In the process of gathering Alaska caribou legends and stories, I learned that the native people in fact do not migrate with the caribou, as the Sami people do with the reindeer. The caribou nevertheless are central to the lives of many indigenous people in Alaska, and certain groups mark their calendar year according to the migrations. Like the reindeer, the caribou are threatened by industrial powers and incursions into their territory as oil companies buy up the land across which the caribou migrate. Keith and I shared the people's sorrow and concern about this threatened species, and we left Alaska with renewed reverence and awe for the beauty and the sacredness of the Arctic wilderness and the precious animals that live there.

In the spring of 1992, I heard that an international conference on shamanism would be held in Siberia. Since I was already scheduled to give some lectures in Eastern Europe and Russia and going to Siberia had been a lifelong dream of mine, I made inquiries about traveling there. Now I especially wanted to go because by this time I had learned about several different nomadic Siberian tribes that follow the reindeer. But Russia at that time was in chaos. Neither American travel agents nor Intourist, the official Russian travel service, could help me arrange a trip to meet the reindeer people, nor could they understand why I would want to depart from the usual travel sites to visit an obscure group of people. Moreover, I had to obtain a special government visa permission, accounting for every day I spent in any Russian province.

By "chance," I mentioned my Siberian dream trip to one of my best friends. She suggested that I contact a Siberian woman who was then staying with one of her relatives. This woman's husband turned out to be a travel agent in Siberia as well as a former scientist. Not only could he make travel arrangements for me and obtain an invitation to the shamanism conference, but he knew how to find out where the reindeer people were and how to meet with them. He arranged for us to meet a connection to the tribe in Yakutsk, a town in the province of Yakutia, in the far northeastern sector of Siberia.

So Keith and I followed the Reindeer Woman to Russia. Traveling in Russia during this tense period, even with a guide and interpreter, was an enormous challenge. At several airports in isolated Siberian cities such as Ulan-Ude, we were told that our flight had been canceled due to lack of fuel. Sometimes we were given no information about the cancellation and were told that we would have to wait days to fly out. This meant we might not arrive at Yakutsk in time to make connections to meet the reindeer people.

Invariably, our guide managed to get us from place to place with bribes and convoluted plane and train routes. We experienced the despair of the Russian people as we saw the effects of pollution on their beloved land, the value of the ruble shrinking day by day, and the unpredictability of life in Russia. To meet up with the reindeer people seemed an almost impossible challenge to us by now.

En route to Yakutsk, we were able to visit shamanic sites and take a few days' rest, which helped us reconnect with the spirit of the land and feel the wonder of the journey. We spent a wonderful night on a small boat floating on the deepest lake in the world, Lake Baikal, lying onboard, watching the moon and stars. At a dacha we bathed in a Russian *banya,* had steaming water poured over our bodies, and were brushed with a leafy branch of the holy birch. Our bodies and spirits were renewed after a few days.

By the time we actually reached Yakutsk and boarded a cargo helicopter formerly used by the Soviet military, we had surrendered all our Western preconceptions about control. The helicopter would drop us off near the Arctic Circle in the remote mountainous region east of the Lena River in wild Yakutia. Sitting on sacks of potatoes in the noisy helicopter with a few of the native people, and looking at the majestic country below, we thanked the divine forces for our good fortune in finding our way to reindeer country.

After several hours, the helicopter swooped down between two mountain ranges and landed in the middle of a nearly dry, rocky riverbed. We jumped from the helicopter to the ground with Galina, our Russian interpreter, and Ivan, our wilderness guide, as some of the nomadic Even came running down a hill to greet us. They were carrying reindeer meat for the pilots who had brought them these strange visitors. When the helicopter flew off, we briefly wondered whether the gas shortage would keep it from returning to pick us up. Would we be stranded in this wild and beautiful but eerie Arctic wildland? We could see from their faces that

Galina and Ivan had their doubts, too. But one of the Even motioned for us to come with them, and we were reminded of the purpose of our journey.

We followed the clanspeople up a hill to an open mountain valley, where we were greeted by the Even community and their elder. Here, in the middle of the Siberian mountains, the Even had camped for a several-day pause on their long annual journey. They had been visited by foreigners only twice before as they followed the reindeer through the wilderness—once by two European hunters who stayed for only one day, and once by a BBC crew that had filmed them.

The elder grinned at us and pointed in the distance. There hundreds of reindeer were running toward us, with a sea of antlers that looked like birch branches moving in the wind. Their hooves thundered on the tundra, as mothers and calves grunted calls to one another. Suddenly the surging herd stopped some thirty yards away from us, and we saw that riders atop some of the reindeer were guiding the herd. More than thirteen hundred reindeer were there, the elder proudly told us.

The Even are among the most ancient of Siberian tribes, and they now are one of the smallest clans that still observe age-old traditions centered on reindeer. They are hunters and fishers as well as nomadic reindeer herders. The elder, a short round man of seventy, emanated the wisdom and beauty of a Buddha. He spoke to us about his people's beliefs, saying that the Even people need the reindeer, just as the reindeer need them—the souls of the people and the reindeer are interrelated and interdependent. Each Even person has a special relation to a particular live reindeer that is his or her spirit guide. As he told us this, he pointed to a nearby tree and said that this earthly tree was an embodiment of the world tree, and that the antlers of the reindeer comprised its branches. When an Even dies, the corpse is placed in a coffin and hung high among the branches of a tree, along with the antlers of that person's special spirit reindeer. In the leafy cradle of this transforming "tree of life," the Even believe, the souls of the human and the reindeer return to the spirit world together, where people and reindeer still ride as they do on earth.

Without a reindeer, a living Even person is not a human being, the elder told us, since the people's nature is half-human, half-reindeer. In a deep spiritual sense, the Even people feel that they *are* reindeer and that the reindeer communicate with them. Reindeer show them the best pastures and communicate with divine forces—with the mountains, the rivers, and the winds; they know where the other animals are. In their living mythology the Even believe that the reindeer will carry them into the future. Thus, the elder said, the Even people are very worried about the fate of the reindeer, since their existence and habitat are now threatened by pollution.

When the Soviets were in power they neither valued nor understood nomadic ways of life and enforced restrictions on the Even that resemble nineteenth-century U.S. policies for Native Americans. These bureaucratic constraints are destructive to indigenous lifeways. Many Even people were confined to certain districts, from which they were not supposed to travel to be with one another. This frustrates their nomadic nature and their life purpose, which is to follow the ever-journeying reindeer across earthly regions as well as spiritual realms. Many of the tribal people who live in cities have forgotten how to take care of reindeer.

Before the Even were forced into these settlements, shamans protected the reindeer and could mediate between their spirits and the people. But after the 1917 revolution, as both the Even elder and other experts in shamanism told us, the Soviet government made a concerted effort to find and kill all the shamans and destroy their ritual vestments. Sorrowfully, the elder told us that his father had had a larger reindeer herd and knew more about caring for reindeer than he himself did, and that he feared that his own children would have even less knowledge and spiritual connection to the animals.

Sitting around the campfire day by day and talking with the people, we learned that the Even believe they were created to ride the reindeer. As they ride the reindeer, they balance themselves and guide their mounts by touching the earth with a large stick. The pole is said to be the world tree that unites the three planes of reality—the upper spirit world, the midworld of earth, and the underworld. The riding pole is more than an ordinary stick, and the balance they achieve transcends sheer physical balance. The pole gives them a supernatural center of balance, through which they experience an ecstatic state of serenity. Riding the revered antlered animal is a spiritual experience. "The reindeer is a child of the sun," one of the Even teachers told us, "and turns into a great swan as it flies to the sun, which is its home. A golden reindeer pulls the sun across the sky. When we ride the reindeer, we fly like birds. To us, the reindeer is like a great spaceship, a great bird that is always in the air."

As we lived with the Even people, surrounded by the mystical and actual presence of the reindeer; as we listened to their living mythology, drank the holy milk of the *vaja,* the female reindeer, ate its meat, and even drank its fresh warm blood, we drifted into another sense of time and space. We climbed the mountains above the valley, walked along the high ridges, and felt the warm touch of the sun, their mother, on our skin. Our hearts were caressed by the people and the reindeer and by nature's generosity. The vibrant colors of the late summer tundra—the red and yellow bushes, the muted green and golden mosses, and the lavender cast of the lichen-covered gray rocks—intermingled with the ever-swaying antlers of the deer.

On the afternoon of our arrival, Keith went hiking on the mountain ridge above the camp, where he had a vision of the same Reindeer Woman he had seen in his dream. Overwhelmed by the presence of the goddess, he bowed to honor her. The next day, Keith told the tribe of his vision and his previous dream. The dream and vision had a serious meaning to the Even since they worship a dark-skinned reindeer goddess. Her name, Khinken, means "without stress" and she is protectress of the animals and of all living things. When she appears to one of the Even in a dream, they will be successful in their next hunt, they believe. Although our friends had not told us that they would hunt that night, *they* knew, upon hearing of Keith's dream and vision, that the reindeer goddess had promised them success in hunting.

That night it was so cold that I couldn't sleep. Early in the morning I arose to warm myself by the campfire. When I reached the fire three severed heads of bighorn sheep lay before it. The heads were bloody, and the bighorns' eyes stared out at me. The clan had been hunting. To my surprise, I was neither frightened nor appalled. The huge animal heads, I recognized, were simply part of an organic whole. As I stood by the fire and looked into the bighorns' eyes, the elder came out of his tent and, nodding to the sheep with a big smile, said, "Good."

Later, the chief hunter told us that they had ridden their reindeer in the mountains that night for three hours. The reindeer had showed them where the bighorn sheep were and signaled them to wait. They waited until the reindeer indicated it was time. Then they dismounted from the reindeer, he said, and the wild sheep came to them to be caught.

On the day we left the Even, the elder told us: "We are glad that at last Russia and America are peaceful friends. We roamed with the reindeer during the Communist–Stalinist period and let the whole antagonism pass by. And now finally we have peace. In our language, we do not use the word *kill* because that word means to kill the soul. We believe that all peoples have different ways to the spirit and that each way is good like the different cells in the body."

As we waited for the helicopter that was to take us back to the city, in my heart I hoped it would not arrive. I did not want to leave this Siberian Shangri-la, the elder, or the beautiful, gentle Even people. Most of all, I couldn't bear to leave the reindeer—their wild and soulful eyes, their astonishing antlers that beckoned to other worlds. But even if fate did not allow me to return to this place in the wilderness, to see the reindeer another time, I knew that their miraculous presence was now engraved deeply in my heart. I felt certain that the reindeer and the people who follow them would visit me in my dreams. And I wanted to share the message of their beauty and transformative power with others.

Two

SPIRIT GUIDE

hen I was a child, I could hardly wait until Saturday mornings, when Dolly would appear. Dolly was an old white horse that pulled a milk wagon through Philadelphia's cobbled stone streets. Rushing out to greet her, I would throw my arms around her neck, then stroke her nose and touch her soft velvet mouth gently with my left hand, which held the sugar cube she loved so much. After Dolly nuzzled me, the driver signaled her to continue on their delivery route. Every Saturday I followed Dolly faithfully through the narrow streets and alleys, praising her with pats, apples, and carrots at her stops. When she passed into the district where my mother had forbidden me to go, I followed Dolly with my eyes until I could see her old white back no longer. All the rest of the week, I accompanied her spirit with my heart, always wondering where she went when I could not go with her, hardly able to wait until the next Saturday, when I could be with her again.

One Saturday, neither Dolly nor the milk wagon appeared. In tears I asked my mother what had happened. I don't remember what my mother told me, but eventually I learned that Dolly had died. The horse-drawn milk delivery service was canceled, and a motorized milk truck took its place. Hard black asphalt replaced the old cobblestone streets, and at night electric lights were substituted for the warm golden gas streetlights that had made our bleak neighborhood seem a little friendly.

As a little girl growing up poor in the middle of a big city, Dolly was the only horse I encountered. She became my first actual spirit guide. The ritual of following the old white mare every Saturday morning sustained me through the week and gave me hope during my traumatic childhood. No matter how frightened I was on the nights my father came home drunk, I felt the spirit of Dolly and called upon her loving energy to help me. Following Dolly was healing to my small child's suffering soul. Walking faithfully behind her gave me solace. When she disappeared, I felt bereft. Finally, with the help of books, I found fictional horses and other animals who became my friends, and I learned to follow them in my imagination. Without Dolly or her storybook successors like Flicka, Lassie, Black Beauty, the Yearling, and the Black Stallion, I wonder how I could have survived childhood.

Half a century later in the Siberian wilderness, when I was learning from the Even people that each member of their tribe had a special reindeer that was his or her personal spirit guide during this earthly life, I remembered Dolly. How lucky I was to have received this rare gift of nature in the midst of a large impersonal city. As the reindeer are for the Even people, Dolly was the first spirit guide on my young soul's journey.

Following Dolly taught me how important it is to care for an animal friend. From the old mare I learned about love and death and healing. As she pulled the wagon that brought us milk, the liquid equivalent of a mother's nourishing love, I drank in her loving spirit in much the way that the Even people do when they sip the heavenly liquid that the elder women milk from the holy reindeer doe.

A spirit guide can draw us to and along our spiritual journeys—our process of consciously trying to live a reverent life. Just as we sometimes need guides to point the way on our travels through the physical world, on any inner journey of transformation we need trailblazers who encourage us to continue on our quest and who give us direction.

While I was writing this chapter and pondering the meaning of spirit guides, I was on a plane flying to Minneapolis to give a lecture. In the row ahead, I noticed a beautiful blond dog sitting on the floor by the aisle seat. For a moment I questioned my perception, but when I looked again, I saw that the golden retriever was a guide dog accompanying a handsome young blind man. The dog licked the man's hand as he fondled the animal's ears. Here was a living example of a spirit guide. Like the traveling blind man, who needed the guide dog in order to negotiate his way safely, so, at times, all of us need a pathfinder to show us the direction on our life quests.

My mother's real-life animal guide was a huge Saint Bernard dog named Barney, a constant companion who used to go out and find her father on the nights when he failed to come home after a hard night's drinking.

My grandmother, who raised me, told me she had had many spirit guides with whom she conversed—the birds, the deer, the foxes, and the squirrels, even snakes and fish, all the animals that roamed around the farmlands where she grew up. Her special animal guide was an owl that nested in an old oak tree and with whom she would consult, especially on moonlit nights.

My father, who grew up in the city, often told me how much the relationship between the human heroes and the wolf-dog spirit guides portrayed in Jack London's novels had inspired him to survive after his father made him quit school at thirteen to go to work.

Some of us, like my father, find helping guides as we read the pages of a novel, when we listen to a fairy tale, while we watch a film, or in our dreams at night. Animals often appear in literature as symbols of redemption. For instance, in Dostoyevsky's novel, *Crime and Punishment,* a spirit guide appears in a dream to the protagonist, Raskolnikov.

Raskolnikov thinks himself superior to ordinary people and above human morality, and he murders an old woman to try to prove it. He chooses this particular woman as his victim because she is reputed to be mean and abusive to others, and he tries to justify killing her by telling himself that he is ridding the world of a bad person. During his attack on the old woman, her sister sees him, and in his fear and confusion he kills her as well.

Instead of feeling justified and liberated, however, Raskolnikov suffers guilt. He falls sick for three days, during which he is beset with nightmares. In one dream, he is a young boy of twelve and is with his father. He sees a crowd watching a cart man beat an old nag mercilessly when she can no longer pull the overloaded wagon. Unable to bear this cruelty, Raskolnikov runs to the old mare and, throwing his arms around her neck, screams to the cart man to stop beating her. He awakens from the dream sobbing with love and mercy for the weak and bloody horse. The image of the beaten horse in his dream helps Raskolnikov to recover his human feeling by guiding him to the knowledge that he himself has been like the abusive cart man. In his heart he realizes he loves and wants to protect the old mare. Thus her animal spirit draws him toward transformation from his abstract dehumanized theory of being a superman, above human morality, to compassion for living beings.

Every child wants an animal to love, and just as the cart horse reminded Raskolnikov of his feelings, animals teach us how to love. As reindeer are spiritual pathfinders for *all* of the Even people, so in childhood animals are our spirit guides. As children, our hearts went out to Bambi when the hunters, who wantonly intruded upon the forest, brutally shot to death the fawn's mother. Bambi's survival became the hope of many children. Yet somehow, as adults, many of those very children who loved Bambi now sneer at others' love and concern for animals and dismiss their beloved childhood stories and animal heroes and heroines as sentimental. In this way, they scorn the qualities of vulnerability and the open heart.

To follow the deer as a spirit guide requires trust and childlike innocence. Young children who grow up in relatively healthy conditions often have the simplicity to open their hearts to healing images. For example, Martin, who attended one of my workshops on the reindeer spirit, related the following experience. When he was four years old, he was taken to the hospital to undergo surgery. He was afraid to leave home and especially to leave his mother. Just before the operation, Martin remembers, he saw in his imagination a beautiful reindeer, which comforted him and told him that he would recover and return to his family. Even now, as an adult in midlife, Martin calls upon this image of the healing reindeer spirit to give him solace and hope whenever he feels troubled. Just as the reindeer image helps Martin, who grew up in a healthy home, so learning to love and care for animals can help abused children find comfort and empathy.

The temptation to be cynical about the love for animals, and cynicism's threat to the soul's progress, is made clear by Father Zossima, the spiritual mentor and elder in Dostoyevsky's *The Brothers Karamazov:* "Love the animals: God has given them the rudiments of thought and joy untroubled. Do not trouble it, don't harass them, don't deprive them of their happiness, don't work against God's intent. Man, do not pride yourself on superiority to the animals; they are without sin, and you, with your greatness, defile the earth by your appearance on it, and leave the traces of our foulness after you —alas, it is true of almost every one of us!"[1]

The reindeer people—and other indigenous peoples— understand instinctively the truth of Dostoyevsky's maxim: that respect and love for animals yields a humility essential to the soul's journey. Indigenous peoples often directly experience how reverence for animals can flow naturally from life and be part of human survival, an impulse that the naturalist and conservationist E. O. Wilson calls biophilia—the love for other living beings. This view is also expressed by Frank Waters in his novel about Pueblo Native American Indian life, *The Man Who Killed the Deer:* "Nothing is simple and alone. We are not separate and alone. The breathing mountains, the living stones, each blade of grass, the clouds, the rain, each star, the beasts, the birds and the invisible spirits of the air—we are all one, indivisible. Nothing that any of us does but affects us all."[2]

My grandmother shared this philosophy with me when I was a little girl. Even faraway "fantasy" creatures like the reindeer carried a spiritual significance to her. I remember sitting on her lap while she read poems and stories like "The Snow Queen," in which a reindeer helps a young heroine, Gerda, journey to a faraway realm to save her friend, then carries the reunited couple back to their home. Tales like this nurtured my imagination and gave me hope during dark times when I felt constricted and menaced. Reindeer seemed like magical wild horses, whose winglike antlers guided them through the heavens to other worlds—exciting realms of freedom, adventure, love, and generosity. They seemed natural extensions of Dolly, the cart horse. In my fantasies, Dolly, too, had secret wings that bore her through the skies at night after she had finished delivering milk.

When Gram told me about the reindeer, as we sat on the back steps of our cramped row house, her eyes would shine. Telling the stories rekindled happy memories of her own adventures with deer and the other animals that she met on her wanderings through the woods near the farm on which she grew up. Feeling her excitement, encircled by her warm arms, and looking into her loving eyes, I was drawn to dream and hope for better times.

Years later, when I left home and traveled west, I settled in a mountain town to write for a daily newspaper. With my first earnings, I bought a horse, a big, black, shaggy cow pony who became a spirit guide for me in early adulthood and with whom I had many adventures. On weekends, Snooks and I would ride far away, usually into Phantom Canyon, a wild and twisting stretch of land that wound through a narrow, red rocky gorge cut by a roaring river. After a few hours' ride down the canyon, we would settle in an open grassy meadow by the stream, where Snooks grazed and I leaned against an ancient cottonwood tree, thumbing through my well-worn copy of *Walden* to continue my rambles with Thoreau. Decades later in 1986, when Keith told me his dream, old memories of Snooks, and of Dolly and Gram, and my lifelong love of animals, mingled with the image of the Reindeer Woman as a spirit guide.

In the Arctic the shamanic peoples who live according to the rhythms of animals regard the reindeer as a spiritual messenger who travels between heaven and earth, transporting the shaman to the spirit world, where he gathers wisdom to bring back to help heal the community. The reindeer also carry the souls of the dead to the spirit world for rebirth. I wondered whether there was an original spiritual link between reindeer and Christmas imagery.

Our commercial culture sentimentalizes reindeer as Santa's bearers of material objects in our profit-ridden society. Suppose, instead, that Santa were a modern-day shaman, and that his reindeer were ridden by the ancient shamans through the heavens, the antlered angels that guided them to find ways of healing and wisdom from the spirit world. When reindeer become shamanic messengers for peace rather than mundane bearers of presents, their image, so magical to children, takes on spiritual significance.

Buried in the artificial cartoon image of Santa and his reindeer lie traces of ancient shamanic beliefs. The winter solstice was observed and celebrated long before Christmas became a holy day, always with colorful gifts to ward off the darkness of winter. Shamans, like our modern Santa, were said to travel through chimneys in their journeys to the other world. Santa, our modern shaman, cares for the reindeer all year long, until he journeys with them into our hearts, a spirit guide to keep hope alive for us. The gifts brought by the reindeer—who can survive the ravages of winter—help us make it through another winter too; the gifts are spiritual offerings, symbols of transformation for living in harmony with the cosmos. The Christ child can be thought of as a shaman and healer who bridged the human and divine realms. The holy child was born, spirit made flesh, not in the spring—the more usual season for birth in the natural world—but in the middle of winter, a harbinger of peace and our connection with the divine.

Today our artificial view of animals and our subordination of them to ourselves have caused many of us to lose our natural ability to encounter animals in an open way and to partake in the mysteries and the powerful energies that they possess. In a zoo, where cages mentally and physically protect us from animals, we often merely look at the beast without really seeing it. But animals watch us, too. Whoever has trekked freely in nature, unprotected by weapons or other artificial devices, knows the thrill, the threat, the startle, at suddenly meeting the eyes of an animal. The visual act of returning an animal's look may make us become suddenly aware of ourselves in a physical and mystical sense. We may suddenly recognize a wilderness within our souls that mirrors the wildness of a fellow creature. The tribes of the reindeer people look directly into the eyes of the deer and know that the animal has secrets it can reveal to them, knowledge relevant to their own existence, purpose, and survival. If we allow ourselves to look into the eyes of animals with open minds, we, too, will feel awe before their mystery.

Our own reflection framed within the peaceful eyes of the reindeer can remind us of our intimate, primal connection with and responsibility to all of nature. The reindeer's ability to survive the starkest winters and find their way through dangerous wilderness to create new life may help us reclaim a guiding symbol for our existence, one that can help us rediscover and redeem our own enduring instincts. The reindeer can again become spirit guides for us, images of hope and peace that can inspire us to honor and affirm life and peacefully transform ourselves and our world.

Three

CREATION'S
HEARTBEAT

he poet W. H. Auden understood the spiritual power of the reindeer. In his poem, "The Fall of Rome," he intimated the end of the world in the decline of Western civilization. He portrayed our anxiety, despair, and alienation in the modern city; our sense of abandonment in an impersonal society; the inequalities of wealth and the injustices that humiliate us; and our futile attempts to adapt, escape, or rebel. Unexpectedly, out of this darkness, the poet offers us an image of illumination. Our hope, he suggests, lies with the reindeer in the wilderness. The following lines conclude the poem:

> Altogether elsewhere, vast
> Herds of reindeer move across

Miles and miles of golden moss,
Silently and very fast.[1]

The image of reindeer moving in the wilderness points to the possibility of survival and a rebirth of trust and confidence. Nothing except extinction can stop the reindeer in their purposeful annual migration. The image emphasizes the saving grace of silence, space, and solitude. It gives us a vision of another realm, one not yet infected by despair, in which we, too, might move forward with freedom.

When life gets out of balance, the combined forces of nature and the psyche always signal us that something is wrong. They can also lead us back to our true paths from which we have gotten lost. Sometimes an outer event, like Chernobyl, shocks us into awareness; at other times an inner image, such as that in Auden's verse or in a "big dream," emerges spontaneously from the psyche and calls us on a pilgrimage to find our deeper meaning—the unique way we are to follow in our life. When an image has a numinous energy that resonates within us, it draws us to a new potentiality or to a renewed intention, emotion, or value. It can transcend the individual and reach out to humanity's universal core. The ancient peoples of the North see in the earthly reindeer the same archetypal potency of Reindeer Spirit as Auden. They understand that the animal's energy, and all that it embodies, is important in their earthly lives and in whatever exists beyond mortal limits.

Imagine the reindeer—wanderers adorned with crowns; messengers that travel between earth and heaven like angels; survivors that traverse the Arctic wilds each year to deliver life; magical beings that delight our children's creative fantasy and draw the sleigh of Santa Claus, winter's wise old shaman who bequeaths us gifts of transformation beneath the boughs of evergreen trees. Such images can help heal our despair and give us hope in the devastation of our ecological dark night.

In the darkness of our restricted modern lives, we need new visions that can open up our hearts and give us a hopeful metaphor by which to live. The poet and mystic Theodore Roethke once wrote that in a dark time, the eye begins to see. We turn to the shamans, the mystics, and the visionaries who seek unity and harmony with all creation. In our age of crisis, turning to the inner wisdom of the seer may be the most practical, down-to-earth thing we can do. Seeing the earth as one dwelling place for all living beings and caring for that common ground is a necessity if we are to survive.

Today we search for sacred spaces in which we can move freely, according to our nature. Our search is spiritual and physical, and the regions that beckon to us are wilderness— the vast and empty areas where silence and solitude allow original vision. Instead of the archetypal stories of possession of the land and of conquest of other peoples, by which our cultures have defined themselves and by which we have lived, we need to create a new, more compassionate and caring myth to live by, one of reverence for nature. We need to relearn the earth's cosmic melodies and follow its rhythms, as the Sami and the Even people follow the reindeer. Under-standing the ways of the people who follow the reindeer may be part of a "new story" for the next century, a story of redemption that many of us just now are beginning to write. Perhaps if we can release the reindeer spirit inside ourselves, we can learn to run freely across the land without possessing it.

The Sami people's ancient story of creation is a vision of the peace and harmony we seek. Creation myths tell us of our spiritual origins. They herald the beginning of our human journey and point to the meaning and purpose of our lives. They show us the basic truths of the cosmos and help us awaken to our own nature and to the nature of the world.

The importance of the emotion and act of caring is a theme of creation myths from Lapland. Caring is at the heart of all creation. According to an ancient Lapp legend, the first beings that were created in the universe were the reindeer. After these wondrous creatures were set upon the earth, humans were created so that they could follow the reindeer and tend to them. The reindeer, in turn, provided a livelihood for human beings. The purpose of these two—humans and reindeer—was to take care of each other.[2] Caring—reverence for the sacredness of life—gives existence its essential meaning. The following creation myth from the Swedish part of Lapland shows how the caring heart beats at the center of all existence:

Once, while walking in solitude by the eternal waters, the creator, Jubmel, found the peace disturbed by evil spirits. Mocking cries, shrieks of hatred, and evil chants invaded the calm of the eternal void. Disturbed, Jubmel decided to create a new world, a universe so peaceful and harmonious that love and compassion would reign and the evil spirits would flee. He wanted the beautiful body of his favorite creature, a gentle reindeer doe, to be the matter from which the new world would be shaped, and he wanted her loving heart to inform the new creation. So he called the lovely vaja, *the reindeer doe, from Passevaari, the holy mountain upon which she grazed. As the radiant reindeer doe came running, her golden hooves sparkled like shafts of sunlight, delighting the creator's heart.*

Turning to the gentle vaja, *and looking into her tender eyes,*

Jubmel said: "You, my little vaja, *have infinite sadness in your eyes: and from your body I will shape the world to set my Savioaimo (the home of holiness) apart from the nether regions." So the creator took a tiny bone from the body of the reindeer doe and built a bridge that spanned the abyss between the light world and the nether regions.*

The innermost structure of the new earth was fashioned from the vaja*'s bones and became the rocks and boulders and the peaks and mountain ridges. Her flesh became the fertile soil, and her blood and veins the flowing rivers. From her hair the mysterious forests were created. Her skull became the sky, which shields the earth from the blazing brightness of the holy heavens. The reindeer's deep, sad eyes became the morning and the evening stars to guide the songmakers, the dreamers and the parted lovers and to give them hope.*

Finally, Jubmel hid the vaja*'s still-beating heart in the centermost depths of the earth to remind the lost wanderer, the lonely mountaineer, and all those in sorrow, that help would always be there. The* vaja*'s heart would be the heartbeat for the earth, so that when peace and love reigned the reindeer doe's heart would beat with joy. But if hatred and greed disrupted the earth's harmony, her heart would convulse in pain and tremors would shake the earth from top to bottom.*

The beauty of the new earth was abundant. Sweet milk—the holy milk of the vaja*—flowed forth from the rivers. The tree trunks were filled with marrow, and cheese-fruit and meat-fruit hung from the branches of the birch and the firs. Jubmel asked the sun to shine upon this wondrous creation, and the splendid world created from the body of the gentle reindeer doe was so warm and loving that the evil spirits could not approach it.*

Delighted with the new world, Jubmel wanted to share his joy, so he decided to create beings of his own kind to rejoice on the earth.

From a small, nameless substance, Jubmel shaped two men to be children of the earth and asked his son, Beijve, the sun god, to warm the earth and guard and love it. In turn, Beijve asked the new beings to care for the earth and its gifts—the fleet-footed reindeer, the fruit-bearing trees, and all its wonderful treasures. The only commandment Jubmel gave them was not to hate.

At first the brothers loved each other and dwelt upon the earth in peace. They sang with joy and gratitude while, deep in the earth, the reindeer doe's heart beat with love. Hearing the earth's glad music, Jubmel and Beijve smiled with holy joy. Jubmel had another son, Mano, who, after he rebelled against his father, had been cast out from Savio-aimo, the heavenly realm. When Mano saw the two new beings living so peacefully, he wanted to make trouble. So, he whispered wicked words to one of the earth-brothers as he was sleeping. From that moment on, this brother, Attjis, became restless and left home. The other brother, Njavvis, grieved at this loss. But he was comforted when he listened to the holy vaja's *heartbeats deep in the earth.*

Filled with compassion for the abandoned Njavvis, the sun god, Beijve, shed a great tear. From this loving, tender tear of compassion and the sun god's gentle, joyous smile, Jubmel created the first woman to be a mate for Njavvis. From this couple, a race of happy, sun-bright people—the Samis—would be born. The first woman's eyes were the color of Jubmel's beloved and shyest flower, the sky-blue gentian, and held the mystery of love and life and hope. Her forehead was pure, high, and free. Her voice was sweet and as musical as the song bird, and her name was Njavvis-ene. Then Njavvis thanked Jubmel for creating such a wondrous woman.

But as soon as Attjis heard her voice and saw his brother's beautiful soul mate, he craved her. Envy and bitterness overwhelmed Attjis, and he ceased listening to the guiding, loving heartbeats of the reindeer doe in the center of the earth. Then the evil Mano called forth his own daughter with black magic and chants and gave her to the envious Attjis as a mate. From then on, the envious Attjis was never satisfied with what he received, and he demanded from his generous brother, Njavvis, more and more land, which in his greed he abused. Finally, Attjis became so possessed by evil spirits that he beat his brother to death with the head and antlers of a slain deer. In horror, Beijve withdrew the sun, and the reindeer doe's wounded heart throbbed so hard that the earth rocked violently and flung the wicked brother up to the moon.

Meanwhile, children had been born to both couples, engendering a race of human beings in which evil increased. The humans found no joy in the peace and plenty that the creator had given through the body of the reindeer doe, and they began to take all the good things from the earth without thanksgiving. As a result of these cold-blooded acts, the heart of the creator's vaja, *buried in the earth's center, trembled with terror at so much wickedness, so that the upper earth quaked and many people fell into the chasms. Jubmel decided to reverse the world and to destroy this wicked race, and he turned the sea waters on the land so the greedy people would perish.*

Seeing all the suffering, Njavvis-ene, now a goddess in the heavens called Beijen-neite,[3] entreated her father, the sun god, to help the dying earth people. In turn, he pleaded with Jubmel, who helped the two last humans, a boy and a girl, to survive by placing them asleep on the holy mountain of Passevaari. And Beijen-neite made the earth a beautiful place once more so the children would be greeted by the birds, animals, and flowers when she awakened them with warm and loving kisses.

The heart of humankind, Jubmel thought, is strange, for it sneers at godly gifts in times of joy and plenty. So to save this peculiar race from itself and to part the light from the darkness, the creator hid all the marvelous treasures of the earth—gold and silver, milk and cheese-fruit—deep in the midearth, near the heart of the holy vaja. *But he relented and allowed some of the rich milk to remain on earth, hiding it in the udder of the female reindeer.*

From then on, the new people, born later to the two remaining earth-children, had to wander to seek the gifts buried near the heart of the holy reindeer doe. They had to struggle to live from the earth, for the former riches had been hidden. In their sleep, they had forgotten how the world had been shaped from the body of the gentle reindeer doe. Nor did they know of the treasures hidden near her heart. So Beijen-neite returned to the earth to be near them. Sometimes she allowed herself to be seen, and sometimes she came in the form of a reindeer. She taught them the ways of goodness and humility, and how to tame the wild deer and to make clothes and shelter from it. Warmed by the loving care of the sun-mother, Beijen-neite, they became the Sami (Sameh) people who learned the tales of the hidden treasure from the songs of the shaman and who journey, searching for the peace and harmony that is safe-guarded by the heartbeat of the sacred reindeer doe. To the beat of the magic drum, made of reindeer skin, the shamans still remind the people always to listen for the holy vaja*'s joyful heartbeats. For near her loving, throbbing heart, the treasures of creation are being saved for them.*[4]

As we near the end of the twentieth century and approach the new millennium, the planet is enveloped in a Dark Night of the Soul. As described by mystics, the Dark Night of the Soul is a testing time that occurs when old, customary ways of being have proved inadequate. It is a time of transition that can lead toward a new state of consciousness but that necessitates a period of chaos, torment, and disruption. The darkest of these times can be a threshold to a higher state of spirituality. Mystics like Saint John of the Cross, Rumi, Saint Teresa of Ávila, and Etty Hillesum (a young Jewish woman who personally bore witness to the Holocaust in our century and wrote *An Interrupted Life*) said that these agonizing periods of impotence, depression, and desolation, these painful periods of privation in which we feel abandoned by "God," can be times of divine purgation. The Dark Night provides us with the spiritual opportunity to re-create moral character, purify spiritual life, refine the soul, and receive divine illumination, through which we can progress to higher consciousness.[5]

The mystical poet, playwright, and philosopher Maurice Maeterlinck actually compared the paradox of living through the Dark Night to existence in the North Pole:

> Here we stand suddenly at the confines of human thought, and far beyond the Polar Circle of the mind. It is intensely cold here; it is intensely dark; and yet you will find nothing but flames and light.
>
> But to those who come without having trained their souls to these new perceptions, this light and these flames are as dark and as cold as if they were painted. Here we are concerned with the most exact of sciences: with the exploration of the harshest and most uninhabitable headlands of the divine "Know Thyself": and the midnight sun reigns over that rolling sea where the psychology of man mingles with the psychology of God.[6]

We are living in a time of violence and predatory greed that threatens us with our own extinction and the destruction of all life. Many people, like the creator Jubmel, want to create the world anew so that harmony and peace will prevail. They envision re-creating the world from the gentle heart—from the spirit of the loving reindeer doe, whose body will be the very ground of existence. They understand, however, that along with the gifts of any new creation of harmony comes an element of disharmony that causes disruption. People forget and backslide. At these points teachers like Beijen-neite come to earth to remind humans that the heart of the holy reindeer is in their care, that their fates are intertwined and they must care for each other.

Beijen-neite, created from a beautiful smile and a tear of joy, is the feminine force within ourselves that can inspirit us and teach us the art of caring anew, just as the reindeer people understand that caring for one another and for the animals gives life meaning. So often in life, tears mark a breakthrough, out of which emerges a new way of being, closer to the heart. If we can stay near the heartbeat of the holy *vaja,* we will find a way to live through the World's Dark Night.

We are in the World's Dark Night because we have lost genuineness in our relationships to one another and to the rest of creation. As Martin Buber, the philosopher-theologian who emphasized the importance of respectful relationship, pointed out, instead of having an "I–Thou" relationship—a soul-to-soul connection with other people, animals, Nature, and all beings—Western humans tend to be locked into a manner of calculative thinking that reduces relationships to "I–It"—an objectified alliance constructed out of a need for power and control. When the urge to control predominates and we define ourselves by our power over others, as exemplified by the "I–It" attitude, we lose our innate awe before the mystery of the world. Concomitantly, we lose our spirituality, our sense of there being something greater than ourselves, greater than a desire for power. Without spiritual relationship, we become despondent and feel "heartless."

In contrast to the materialistic, self-referential attitude that predominates in Western society, aboriginal clans of reindeer people participate with the cosmos in a primary spiritual bond. Through their way of life they have an "I–Thou" soul-relationship with one another, nature, and animals. While they depend on animals for food and the practical necessities of survival, a dependence that they acknowledge, their rituals and folk stories help them to live in this paradox. The reindeer image that I have been encountering in my own dreams and in those of people in my workshops calls upon us all to come back into the "I–Thou" relationship.

As Jung pointed out, the spiritual plight of Western civilization is the result of its alienation from the rest of the world. Western people have become ill psychologically and spiritually from their loss of faith and meaning. This illness often manifests itself in extremes: in listless ennui, or in a compulsive, acquisitive materialism. The illness is marked by loss of soul. Slogans, stereotypes that demean others, and facile "how-to-do-it" solutions will not help us regain soul in the long run. We need, instead, a genuine spiritual orientation, one that requires concentrated attention, focused work, and patience, one that has a motivating vision like that of the rejuvenating powers of the reindeer.

In Siberia, I experienced firsthand the vital, healthy soul of the Even people. Their focused attention and their heart-work were always "with" the reindeer whom they tended. I came to use the pronoun *who* when referring to the reindeer, since the Even feel an "I–Thou" soul-relationship with these animals. By following the reindeer, the people's time adjusted to the animals' time; Nature's rhythms became their own tempo. At home in the wilderness, the Even people value visions and wait patiently for the reindeer to reveal their wishes to them.

Prophets, poets, and other visionaries have always known that it is in the wilderness that we find spirit. Christ, Buddha, and Mohammed went alone to the desert, the forest, or the mountains to pray and ask for vision and enlightenment. They traveled inward to the interior wilderness as well, finding renewed strength and inspiration. We, too, need to journey to the wilderness for inspiration to live in the tension of nature and spirit.

The Reindeer Woman is an image for such a journey. The reindeer embodies the enduring birth-giving instinct to keep going, despite vicissitudes and the long winter night. Honored at the winter solstice, the Reindeer Goddess symbolizes our own capacity for affirming spirit in our interior winters and in the ecological winter that we all face in the World's Dark Night. Ancient, and forgotten by most, the Reindeer Goddess and her message are relevant for our own future survival. In these dark times, we need to acknowledge and draw on a new feminine energy—one that is both gentle and caring, not controlling or afraid. We need a feminine force that is wildly ecstatic yet resolute and tenacious enough to move through the World's Dark Night. We need to be conscious, courageous, and patient enough to descend into the psyche's depths to wait for revelation there and accept it.

"For still the vision awaits its time. If it seems slow, wait for it," Jung once advised in his book *Aion*. The waiting place where we find vision is often the confusing wilderness of our interior soul, a psychological abyss where we are stripped of our ego defenses and distractions. This barren space is also a clear space, as in the Arctic tundra, where there is room and time to root ourselves anew and to receive the revelation. Etymologically, the word *abyss* in German, *Abgrund,* means the soil, the ground that is deepest underneath. Plants, all growing things of the earth, root downward; in the depths of the earth it is possible for all life to take root. In the center of our psyche we find our essential being. There, too, at the center of creation, lies the loving heart of the reindeer doe, just as her earthly embodiment feeds upon the plants of the tundra. But, as the Sami creation story shows us, and as with all growing things, the ground must be continually prepared and tilled for things to grow.

Tending to the abyss does not mean only "doing" something in particular but rather attending to life, being there with care and watching with alert and mindful awareness. It requires seeing both dark and light together in their fundamental wholeness, being aware of the fragility of nature, along with its co-creative potential to experience terrors together with bliss, to endure the paradox of despair and faith, to acknowledge dread and hope, to know that the threat of death is linked with the joy of life.

One way that people awaken into the World's Dark Night to retrieve meaning in their lives is through meditation. Others today have joined drumming and chanting groups, which open up the mind and consciousness in expansive ways. The following vision of creation from the heart of a white deer emerged very powerfully for Marisa, a contemporary woman who had been participating in a special chanting and drumming session. Her personal vision, coming from the same universal source of human imagination as the reindeer creation myth and Auden's poem, offers a picture of the cycle of creation from the heart, a reassuring image for a troubled time:

As the drumming sounded, a dark round hole opened in the earth beneath Marisa's feet. She glided down through the dark tunnel until she emerged in daylight to see a vast southwestern vista with snow-capped mountains, rolling desert, and bright blue sky. It was many years ago, and she was sitting in a large meadow. Dozens of Native American people, who were living there, ran toward her with greetings, and a young man made love with her in the sunny field. Then the entire tribe invited her to trek with them into the wilderness. In the center of a great pine forest, she saw a breathtaking white stag with a magnificent rack of horns. The stag stood motionless, towering ten feet tall above them, otherworldly in his calm presence. Marisa saw the deer's heart burst open. From its heart fell all the beings of existence—people, planets, trees, rocks, animals, and stars. She gathered and guided all of them to a high ridge so they could enjoy the immense view of earth.

Marisa began to sense a star form over her head and another star in the earth under her feet. A force bent her backward, and her belly *became* the earth's surface upon which all beings moved. Her head and feet merged beneath her, and both stars met in a blaze of light, while creation continued its existence on the surface of her being. Circle after circle formed, one above the other, over her body. Woman, man, tiger, day lily, child, turtle, pine tree formed a circle. Above them, another circle of stars, stones, little girl, cactus, and puppy formed. Circle after circle of beings changed places, continually evolving. Marisa also changed places in this unfolding while another form took her place as the ground of all being. As the circles evolved, life returned to unfold on her body surface, but it now began to die and was deposited inside her body through her mouth, then was born again from her vagina. The cycles of life, death, and rebirth continued into infinity with great energy, joy, and pulsation. The wheel of life flowed around in endless profusion. Finally, the symphony exploded into one great starburst.

Marisa said she could not adequately describe in words this nonlinear, multidimensional, timeless experience, which sprang spontaneously from her innermost psyche. In her vision, creation began with lovemaking in the wilderness, where all of creation suddenly emanated from the bursting heart of the otherworldly white deer. This creative outpouring was then offered to Marisa to gather up and to guide to a high ridge in the wilderness, where creation itself could enjoy unfettered vision. Finally, the creative process was passed on to Marisa herself in an evolutionary process moving through her own body, which became a channel for the infinite round of life, death, and rebirth.

Marisa's vision of creation from the white deer's heart echoes the theme of the Sami creation myth, that love and care for all of creation are at the center of cosmic evolution. The center of a Navaho sand painting or a Tibetan Buddhist mandala, each made by a shaman in an act of caring for the health of an individual or a community, is the place from which creation and healing emerges. Similarly, creation burst forth from the deer's heart in Marisa's contemporary vision.

Creation story motifs, such as Marisa's, tend to spring forth from the unconscious whenever a person or culture or era is being prepared for change. This change is usually of a spiritual nature, a growth of consciousness necessary for healing, for bringing into balance or wholeness. Passing through one individual's consciousness, a creation story can become a healing image as it is shared with others. Creation from the heart of the deer, as in Marisa's image, emphasizes the need to widen consciousness through heart-work.

For an individual or for a culture, integrating such a vision can take an entire lifetime. Embodying heart-work as the center of our lives is a healing image for our era, which though in the World's Dark Night, is also at a threshold for transformation. But heart-work requires patience, the courage to be vulnerable, and the resolve to journey inward to face our own dark truths. As the poet Rainer Maria Rilke said, "For one human being to love another: that is perhaps the most difficult of all our tasks, the ultimate, the last test and proof, the work for which all other work is but preparation."[7] The reindeer, who gives her heart as the center of the earth, embodies the energy of such work.

If we are ready to wait in the abyss and to know what lies there, we must be ready to acknowledge and face the danger that extinction of the reindeer as a species, as well as all that they stand for, is possible in our time. After the explosion of Chernobyl, thousands of reindeer were slaughtered in case their meat had been contaminated from the fallout that passed over the Arctic. Perhaps Keith's dream, with its portentous message of the woman who ran with the pregnant reindeer to bring birth-giving and healing, even presaged this horrifying event.

Several years later, at the Telluride Film Festival, I saw a film by the Swedish documentarist Stefan Jarl that showed the bloody carcasses of the slaughtered reindeer being removed by helicopter and dumped into the wasteland. The reindeer's survival, and that of the caribou in Alaska, is clearly related to the ecological and spiritual survival of the human race. As the creation myths from Lapland remind us, reindeer symbolize both the mystery of existence and the essential role of humans to care for them. As the earthly creature whose nature is to travel to give birth, as the animal messenger whose spiritual journey links heaven and earth, and as the legendary being whose heartbeat guides creation, the reindeer is pregnant with meaning for those who believe in transformation and in the healing of body and soul.

Remembering the look in the Siberian elder's eyes, I recall his words: "If the reindeer perish, so will we." The eyes of the Even people reflect not only their love of the reindeer but their awe for life and their courage as they live daily with the threat of extinction and the challenge of survival. In an extreme way, they endure the paradox that challenges us all. There, in the silent solitude of the vast tundra, an Arctic abyss or "wasteland" in whose ground the *vaja* reindeer's heart throbs with the healing that Western civilization needs, the reindeer people continue to journey, ever alert to danger yet constantly caring for the sacred deer that guide them on their way through life.

Four

MESSENGERS OF
TRANSFORMATION

ne snowy day in December at dusk, on the day of the winter solstice, I was hiking with a friend on the Enchanted Mesa in the foothills of the Rocky Mountains, near Boulder. Snowflake stars and icicle candles shone from the dark green pine branches as though a heavenly messenger had placed them there to decorate the forest for Christmas. The deep fresh snow muffled our steps as we listened to the winter wind's string concerto. In a flash, two deer appeared on the hill above us, bounding down in a curve of grace and power like sparks from another world. The deer stopped suddenly before us, and the lead doe turned around and gazed straight into our eyes. In silence and awe we looked at her, spellbound by this timeless moment. Then the doe turned to join the other deer, and the two leaped away. In wonder, my friend and I pondered the meaning in this visitation by the deer.

Animals first entered human imagination as messengers, promising magical and oracular wisdom. They were also offered as devotional sacrifices, and they were a regenerating source of food. Ancient peoples believed that an animal could be eaten so that its spiritual energy filled them, and that animals could be tamed to work for them. Among the reindeer people, each reindeer was not only its specific self but also *Reindeer,* the archetypal spirit of the animal. They believed that animals came from over the horizon and belonged *here,* in this world, and *there,* in the other world; they viewed animals as both mortal and immortal. For these people, worshipping an animal and using it for work was not contradictory, because existence is paradoxical and mysterious, not subject only to rules and rational uniformity.

Still, the essential relationship between human and animal was metaphoric for these people, because animals are both like and unlike humans. Because they share something with us, they always remain open, yet they always remain distinct as well. Animals' silence—their lack of language—distinguishes them from humans' capacity for symbolic thought and expression. Yet in lending their name or character to a mysterious quality, animal metaphors were central as the primordial symbols in the human imagination. People who are familiar with animals and who live closely with them, like the reindeer and the Pueblo peoples, accept this paradoxical relationship between humans and animals—a wisdom that we need to recover in Western culture.

In Western civilization, René Descartes's dualistic thought divided soul from body. By asserting, "I think; therefore, I am," he reduced primary reality to ideas of the mind. In contrast, empirical philosophers, such as David Hume, based their view of reality on the external world, and their scientific followers, the behaviorists, reduced animals to machines and attacked the attribution of human characteristics to non-human beings as anthropomorphic. In both of these rational models of the world, animals are viewed as soulless and lacking feelings and significance. Neither model acknowledges the complex relationship between animals and humans; both abrogate the mysterious paradox underlying the essential unity of matter and spirit. As a result of this dualism, both reduce the "I–Thou" relationship between humans and animals to an "I–It" relationship, marginalizing the significance and power of animals. In post-industrial societies this "I–It" attitude has led to treating animals as raw materials, using them as machines, and regarding them as mere productive means to an end, a tendency that was later extended to human workers.

By observing animals as objects and commercially exploiting them—the bison, tiger, and reindeer, to name a few—many species are threatened with extinction. Killing exotic animals to sell as stuffed trophies or to make their body parts into aphrodisiacs, as in the case of the reindeer's antlers and the rhinoceros's horn, or capturing them for zoos where, as passive captives, they wait in artificial cages to be observed by humans, emphasizes our conquest of them and the exotic places they represent, thereby isolating us from them.[1]

Using animals as spectacles and degrading them into banal caricatures of themselves through commercial ventures and advertisements not only violates them, it deprives *us* of their vital role as messengers of transformation.

Many cultures around the world know the value and necessity of the deer as a spirit guide, and many revere and seek to make contact with it through ritual. The Buddha is often pictured with deer and preached his first sermon on mercy and compassion in the Deer Park in Benares. Christ is often portrayed as a deer. In Hindu mythology, the deer is a symbol for the heart chakra. Lakota and Pueblo Native Americans believe that the deer embodies kindness, generosity, and gentleness. For the Huichol people of Mexico, the deer is the most sacred being in the animal world, for it is the intermediary between humans and the gods. The Huichols believe that deer have the power to see into the heart and teach humans to communicate with each other. Just as Arctic peoples find their meaning on earth by following the reindeer, so the Huichols follow the deer spirit as a guide through dangerous passages into direct knowledge of divinity. For these various cultures, the deer is a spiritual pathfinder showing humans the way to meaning.

In the Sami creation story, the shamans help the people find the way to the reindeer doe's heart, buried deep in the center of the earth. There, by the doe's heart, the people discover all of creation's gifts and treasures. In our inner lives, as well, if we follow the deer, we will be led to our heart's vision, values, and genuine desires. By accompanying the deer, we can embark on a journey that initiates us into the depths of spiritual life. Symbolic of the instinctive wisdom of the heart, the deer fascinates us at a deep unconscious level. Its image can lead us to a crucial event through which personal transformation occurs and the soul is rejuvenated.

In actual life or in a dream, when a deer looks us straight in the eyes it is an invitation to awaken, to follow it in harmony. Following the deer's way signifies the start of a search to find our heart's wisdom. Often the deer stands at the edge of the woods or in a clearing in a forest and calls us to enter this unknown realm to discover what we need to know.

Of all animals, the deer uniquely bears the wisdom of the compassionate heart and has the power to teach humans how to heal and to cure others. The sacred deer is graced with the gift of relationship to the sun, the divinities, and all beings on earth. The deer can lead us to wonder at the mystery that although living beings are distinct and different from each other, they are not separate and alone but are interconnected by the greater cosmic pattern of the whole changing energy of creation.

The necessity for respect and awe before the deer's grandeur and dignity is a motif in Christian stories in which Christ is portrayed as a deer. Saint Teresa of Ávila once likened the deer to the spirit of grace through which we are favored with the blessing of divine love, goodwill, charity, mercy, humility, and thanksgiving for the gift of life. In one Christian legend, a hunter is in the forest. Seeing a deer in a clearing, he takes aim and is about to shoot when suddenly, illuminated by the sun shining through the deer's antlers, he sees a cross. Realizing he is standing before a supernatural being, the hunter puts down his gun in humility, whereupon the deer becomes the Christ, who thanks the hunter and christens him Saint Hubertus. In this story, by saving the deer and exercising compassion and humility, the hunter is transformed into a saint.

In another hunting story, Placidus, a pagan known for his kindness and compassion for his fellow human sufferers, sees a magnificent stag while he is hunting. The hunter is astounded when the stag leaps to a high rock, turns to face the man, and says: "Placidus, why do you not follow me into the heights? I am Christ who loves you and whom you serve without yet knowing it. Your offerings and your spirit of justice please me, and that is why I made myself into a splendid stag, to draw you to me.'' Placidus asks the divine stag to show that he is the Christ. The stag becomes immense and merges into radiant light, in which a crucified man with bleeding heart and limbs becomes visible. When Placidus looks again, only the bare rock remains. His soul enlightened by the vision of the supernatural stag, Placidus renounces his given name, gives up everything he possesses, and surrenders himself wholly to the spirit of Christ.[2]

The deer has the power to help us find the way to compassion and the place of spiritual vision. This role is shown in two classic novels: *The Yearling,* which has influenced and touched many young readers, and *The Man Who Killed the Deer,* which depicts Native American life among the Pueblo people. In both stories the protagonist's life is transformed through encountering the truth that the deer spirit offers, so I will explore their main themes and events.

In Marjorie Kinnan Rawlings's novel *The Yearling,* a deer serves as a spirit guide that leads a young boy on his passage into manhood—a journey of spiritual growth that requires the boy, Jody, to accept that life has both tender and harsh aspects. At the beginning of the story, Jody accompanies his father hunting in the swamplands. A rattlesnake bites the father, who, seeing a doe, calls out to his son to shoot the deer for its liver, a folklore remedy for snakebite. Jody shoots the doe, the first deer he has ever shot, cuts out its liver, and puts it on his father's wound. This marks the beginning of Jody's initiation into his maturity. As Jody sees the dead doe's fawn crying out for its mother, even as he starts to take his father home, he cries. His father survives the almost fatal bite, and after his father regains consciousness, Jody pleads to be allowed to rescue the fawn and care for it at home.

His mother protests; she is overworked. She is hardened

from life's struggles and still suffers from the early deaths of her other babies, born before Jody. She treats Jody, her youngest, with detachment, as though she has used up all her love on the ones that came before him; she tends to be hard on him. But Jody's father has a gentle heart that aches for his boy. He wants him to enjoy his childhood while he can, before life's harshness crushes the brevity of youth. He grants his son's wish. So Jody hikes back into the forest to find the fawn and bring it home. The fawn, named Flag for the shape of its sprightly white tail, becomes the center of Jody's life and lightens the harshness of the family's attempts to survive through farming and hunting.

But as Flag grows older, it cannot be contained in their cabin as a pet. Meanwhile, Jody's father is so severely injured in an accident that he is bedridden. The young deer begins to knock things over and get into sacks of grain, eating up the family's scant food supply. Finally one night the yearling gets loose from the lead by which Jody keeps it tied outside and eats the crop of corn upon which the family is depending for the spare winter. Now that the deer has tasted the corn, it will not be possible to keep it away from the family's food supply. The deer is now a threat to their survival.

At a point of crisis in the family, Jody's father orders him to shoot the deer, an act that will symbolize the boy's passage into adulthood. Jody refuses in horror. Angry and desperate, his mother takes up a gun, aims at the yearling, and accidentally wounds it in the leg. She tells Jody that she didn't mean to hurt the creature but wasn't able to shoot straight enough to kill the deer with one shot. When Jody's father orders his son to kill the deer and put it out of its suffering, the weeping boy hopes to rescue the deer but knows he cannot. Finally, after an agonizing internal struggle, he kills the yearling to end its pain.

In bitter anger at his parents, Jody leaves home and spends nights of despair in the swamp. On his return, he is changed. Seeing that his son has taken one of life's hard punishments and survived, that he is no longer a "yearling," Jody's father tells him: "Ever' man wants life to be a fine thing, and a easy. 'Tis fine, boy, powerful fine, but 'tain't easy. Life knocks a man down and he gits up and it knocks him down agin. I've been uneasy all my life. I've wanted life to be easy for you. Easier'n 'twas for me. A man's heart aches, seein' his young uns face the world. Knowin' they got to git their guts tore out, the way his was tore. I wanted to spare you, long as I could. I wanted you to frolic with your yearlin'. I knowed the lonesomeness he eased for you. But ever' man's lonesome. What's he to do then? What's he to do when he gits knocked down? Why, take it for his share and go on."[3]

Jody knows it is now his own turn to accept adulthood and work for the family's survival. But he can't forget Flag, and he wonders whether he will ever be able to love anyone or anything as much as he loved the deer—even his own children. Jody recognizes that he had to kill the yearling in order to fulfill his share of life's obligation, but even so, on the night of his return as he falls asleep, Jody calls out for the deer, crying, "Flag."

In the swamp's darkness, Jody has gone through a Dark Night of the Soul, a necessary passage through despair and into adulthood, a natural psychological experience of maturation, or of dealing with crisis. The Dark Night is analogous to an ancient mythic image, that of the Night Sea Journey, during which the sun is devoured by the sea each night and must endure the darkness before it is reborn. Our human passage is like the sun's; each new day, each phase of growth requires a death of the old self before the new person can be regenerated. Like Jonah, swallowed in the belly of the whale, like the suffering Job, and like all of us who are challenged to come to higher consciousness by struggling through adversity, Jody must consciously undergo the death of his boyhood in order to become an adult.

Transformation requires sacrifice and surrender, a readiness to die for the birth of the new creative being. Readiness for the spiritual journey demands that we relinquish possessiveness and expectation, die to old ways of perceiving, and dare to leap into the unknown. Facing the death of the old self and accepting the sojourn into the Soul's Dark Night is essential to human development. But if we face the pain and death that spiritual growth entails, we will be given courage, consciousness, and compassion. If we struggle through the dark journey, we will return braver, more serene, and psychologically and spiritually enriched.

Having killed the deer, the being that he loves most in the world except for his parents, Jody is faced with one of life's greatest horrors. He has felt the grimy soot from the ashes of his childhood and the purification of his soul, which Saint John of the Cross described in his poem, "The Dark Night of the Soul." Jody has learned that life in the swamp depends on savage acts and the killing of other life for survival. Crossing over a year of transition from innocence to knowledge, Jody now understands and accepts the shooting of the deer as a necessary sacrifice. He is able to forgive his parents for asking him for this sacrifice and is ready to assume the responsibilities of his new stage in life.

Jody's mother, who first shoots the deer, is like a reindeer mother. She will do whatever she must in order to save her family, just as the reindeer mother uses her antlers to protect her young from anything that threatens it. Once Flag has been fully sacrificed, however, the deer becomes an inner image and guide for Jody's passage from adolescence into adulthood. The sacrifice of the deer in *The Yearling*, as spirit guide, has drawn forth the boy's love, thrust him into the crucible of transformation, and prepared him for a spiritual journey that exacts courage and consciousness but can yield wisdom and strength. Survival—physical and spiritual—in the southern swamplands is as challenging as it is in the stark Arctic northlands. The deer helps guide the spiritual crossing from one stage of life to another. By following the deer, which bears the wisdom and power of the healing heart, we can learn how to care for the soul and for the earth.

Frank Waters's *The Man Who Killed the Deer* is another novel in which a deer aids a human being in finding compassion. Here the deer comes to haunt the man who has transgressed natural and ritual laws. Martiniano, the haunted protagonist, is caught between the ancient ritual ways of his native culture and the modern ways of the white man. Taken from his tribe to be educated in the white man's government school, Martiniano returns as a married man to the pueblo, only to find that his parents have died and that he is considered an outcast. Alienated from the white world and from the pueblo, Martiniano dresses in store-bought clothes and shoes, yet braids his hair and wears a blanket like his people. But he has refused to practice the pueblo's ritualistic ways, and so the Council denies him the privileges of other tribe members. One of the community rights he is denied is the use of the community thresher for wheat. Thus, he is disadvantaged in his preparations for the coming winter, and it takes him longer than usual to store his grain. This causes him to be late in going hunting for a deer to feed himself and his wife through the winter.

A government officer catches Martiniano killing a deer two days after the season is over, calls him a "dirty Indian," and kicks him; when he resists, he cracks his head with the side of his gun. In the court of the white man, Martiniano is judged guilty on two counts: killing a deer out of season in the national forest and resisting arrest. When he is sentenced to three months in jail or a fine of $150, a white trader, sympathetic to the peoples of the pueblo, covers the fine in return for payment by work. But the issue of the deer still is not settled, and the Indian Council also brings Martiniano up before its tribunal.

The Council's view on the deer killing is more complicated. To them, Martiniano has ignored the tribal reverence for the deer. By killing the deer without ritual acknowledgment, without the proper ceremonies, without recognizing that its life is as valuable as the hunter's, and without asking for its permission to kill it, he has violated the unwritten tribal code:

In the old days we all remember, we did not go out on a hunt lightly. We said to the deer we were going to kill, "We know your life is as precious as ours. We know that we are both children of the same Great True Ones. We know that we are all one life on the same Mother Earth, beneath the same plains of the sky. But we also know that one life must sometimes give way to another so that the one great life of all may continue unbroken. So we ask your permission, we obtain your consent to this killing."

Ceremonially, we said this, and we sprinkled meal and corn pollen to Our Father Sun. And when we killed the deer we laid his head toward the East, and sprinkled him with meal and pollen. And we dropped drops of his blood and bits of his flesh on the ground for Our Mother Earth. It was proper so. For then when we too built its flesh into our flesh, when we walked in the moccasins of its skin, when we danced in its robe and antlers, we knew that the life of the deer was continued in our life, as it in turn was continued in the one life all around us, below us, and above us.

We knew the deer knew this and was satisfied.

But this deer's permission was not obtained. What have we done to this deer, our brother? What have we done to ourselves? For we are all bound together, and our touch upon one travels through all to return to us again. Let us not forget the deer.[4]

Martiniano's dreams begin to haunt him. He confesses to his wife, Flowers Playing, that the deer drifts into his dreams like a gentle doe or bursts into his thoughts like a rutting buck. He remembers that when he first saw Flowers Playing, her dancing reminded him of a deer. Her graceful movements expressed wild strength; her dreamy brown eyes looked like the soulful eyes of a beautiful doe. One night, as he puts his arms around his wife, he hears a noise at the doorway like the hooves of a frightened or angry spirit deer. Haunted by the sounds, Martiniano withdraws from Flowers Playing and cannot sleep. Later, he cannot forget the sound of the deer, which recurs nightly. Coldness grows between the couple, and Martiniano begins to ignore his wife. He blames the cursed deer for destroying their love, for causing his own lack of faith and the pueblo's rejection of him. Secretly, he feels guilty for the way in which he killed the deer. He hungers for faith, but he can turn neither to the pueblo's kiva, which is closed to him, nor to the white man's church. A controversial native group that uses peyote to find the Red

Road, the road to enlightenment, invites him to join them, so he decides to try the magic plant.

After Martiniano takes peyote, he has a vision of himself in a cornfield. There he thinks that he can take the corn and that people will mistake it for gold, making him rich. But he suddenly realizes that money can't buy the faith he needs. In his vision he then travels to the plains, where he sees racing red stallions. With their power, he feels, he could avenge himself against his people for rejecting him. But a voice tells him: "Power is persecution, not the way to peace." He travels farther, to beautiful blue mountains covered with pine and columbine, but he is so restless, he cannot enjoy this sacred place's peace. Suddenly he sees a deer enter a clearing and out of habit reaches for his gun. But he has forgotten it.

In the peyote vision, the deer stands still and looks straight into Martiniano's eyes. Martiniano admires its strength and beauty but is shocked to realize he is looking at the very deer he has killed—risen from the dead. In fear, he searches for a club. The pine trees around him nod sadly to the deer, and Martiniano suddenly knows that *he* is the intruder in this peaceful place, not the deer. He flees, but the deer chases him; he can feel its hot breath on his back and hear the thunder of its hooves. Racing back through the plains, the cornfields, and into the peyote teepee, Martiniano trembles with terror as he hears the deer race around the tent, beating the earth with its fury.

The night after the peyote vision, Martiniano awakens in fear. Having pawned the skin of the deer he killed, he feels urgently that he needs to retrieve it. He runs to the trader, pleads for the return of the skin, returns home with it, and hangs it on the wall. He is trying to appease the spirit.

After such a vivid vision, Martiniano is somewhat leery of the Peyotee path, but he still participates. On the way to another meeting in the twilight, he hears the bushes snap and a shape moves before him. He recognizes with some fear that it is the deer he killed; it has the same marked skin that now hangs on his wall at home, the same five-pointed antlers, the same great round eyes. Deer and human look straight at each other. He wonders what he should say to the deer; apology seems pointless now. He knows the deer knows his thoughts.

When he tries to move toward the peyote teepee, the deer lifts its antlers, paws the earth, stares at him with ghostly eyes, and leaves no room on the trail for him to pass. "Why doesn't this deer I have killed go about its business and leave me go about mine?" Martiniano mutters in anger. The deer disappears without a sound.

Martiniano fears the peyote is driving him mad and goes home to check whether the deerskin is there. When he sees it, he starts back to the peyote teepee. But once again he cannot go past the spot where the deer stopped him. Martiniano returns home and tells Flowers Playing that he will stop taking peyote. Feeling better, he embraces her; that night he does not hear the deer at his door.

Nevertheless, Martiniano still alternates between faith and cynicism. The deer he killed, then met on the trail, saved him from the harm of peyote, disapproved by the pueblo as a dangerous path to spiritual insight, and restored his happiness with Flowers Playing. Yet it has also brought him trouble and unhappiness. Confused, Martiniano questions his life. He knows that he is caught in a changing time—the pueblo is divided against itself through these changes, and its ancient ceremonies are pitted against the white man's way. The spirit of the deer still haunts him, and he knows he cannot evade it. He realizes that this ephemeral being is a flash of truth in an unbalanced, chaotic world.

Despite his growing spiritual awareness and self-understanding, Martiniano still has trouble. He almost kills a Mexican sheepherder who intrudes into his home. He is publicly punished by the pueblo with fifteen lashes in the plaza, for admitting that he had used peyote, a practice that the pueblo considers harmful to their way of life. The same day of his humiliation, Flowers Playing proudly tells him that she is pregnant with his child. Martiniano feels new tenderness and strength, realizing that life is a mystery that expands beyond the visible.

Martiniano begins to think that he has finally escaped the deer spirit and begins to feel smug, but the deer interrupts his pride: One morning he finds his crop of corn flattened, and he sees the track of a deer hoof and fresh spoor. Angered, he wants to kill the intruders—two does and a buck. But when he aims his gun at them, he cannot fire. The buck has the same five-pointed antlers and skin markings of the deer he killed. He watches the deer's wild gentility, purity, and freedom as they run in the moonlight like supreme beings of the earth. Yet he still cannot accept his own vulnerability and their sovereignty. He curses and blames the deer for deflating his pride, and he swears vengeance on the dead deer.

Every autumn, in a ceremony to celebrate summer's passage, the pueblo honors a deer that gave its permission to be sacrificed for the festival. A dead deer is hung from the top of a pine pole planted in the plaza, and many people climb the ritual pole to try to bring down the deer. This year, no one succeeds. To Martiniano, the deer resembles the one he killed, and he sees the contest as his chance to vanquish the deer spirit forever. He does succeed in climbing the tall pine pole to struggle to bring down the carcass, but his strength fails him. He feels an invisible influence bear down upon him, defeating him again and shattering his pride. Martiniano finally admits humbly that the deer has a power that he can neither overcome nor escape; instead, he must accept it and try to comprehend it.

Flowers Playing reveals a deep connection she has with deer to her tormented husband. She invites him to watch her as she calls the living buck and does to her at dusk. She stretches her arms while the does lick salt from her hands, and a vision overwhelms Martiniano. The deer appear to be gigantic ghostly figures, the mythological beings that his ancestors revered. They become the great animals that gave rise to the Deer Clan, that lent their name to the Pleiades in the heavens, that spread over the earth in countless numbers, that offered their hooves for ceremonial rattles used in every sacred dance, that were friends with the eagle above and the snake below, and that entrusted the mystery of their swiftness, gentleness, and wildness to all human beings. Flowers Playing seems to have become an astonishing Deer Woman with the wild grace that he first saw in her when she danced. He sees Flowers Playing as a woman who is his wife but who also, on another level, is purer and greater than anything he can touch with his human hand—an inviolate, sacred embodiment of the feminine force that holds the mysterious power to attract the hallowed deer. During hunting season, Martiniano sees Flowers Playing call the deer into her corral to help them elude some white hunters. Martiniano's awe of his wife's power with the deer deepens, and he begins to fear her relation to them. He comprehends that she also has a sacred connection to the deer that he killed, the deer that he cannot evade and that continues to haunt him.

In autumn, instead of traveling back to the pueblo with Martiniano in their annual trip down from the mountains, Flowers Playing tells him that she wants to stay longer in the mountains, where she feels most at home, with the changing leaves and the deer. When she does finally return to the pueblo weeks later, she seems to have assumed some of the characteristic elusiveness of the deer. Her large, brown, luminous eyes have a dreamlike quality, her stride an effortless grace, her general demeanor a wildness.

At the winter solstice, Flowers Playing tells him that the pueblo has invited her to participate in the tribal Deer Dance as Deer Mother—a sacred role that recognizes her grace, power, and devotion to the deer. Martiniano feels an awe for her feminine authority that vexes him, yet he accepts that Flowers Playing is more than just his wife; she is the living symbol of an ineffable power held by all women. Tormented and bewildered, he secretly fears that the deer he killed has bewitched his wife and is striking back at him through her. But he knows that he must accept this experience and try to understand it.

On the morning of the Deer Dance, two Deer Chiefs, dressed in white, with antlers branching from their heads, emerge from the kiva, followed by dancers wearing animal skins and holding sticks to serve as forelegs. They move like animals over the fresh snow, from the forest and plains, into the center of the plaza. Two women wearing white buckskin gowns, boots, and eagle feathers in their hair dance with lowered eyes; they emanate the timeless majesty of their sacred being as Deer Mothers. The Deer Mothers move in silent dignity between two lines of animal dancers, while the deer, buffalo, mountain lion, coyote, and antelope personages recede and quiver with low grunts before the inviolable Deer Mother, just as all men must yield to the female charge of creation. They follow the Deer Mother as *She* leads them in great circles and dancing ovals.

As the mothers of all beings, the Deer Mothers dance in

purity commanding the animals in their bond to surrender to this cosmic archaic energy of creation—the force necessary to preserve and perpetuate existence. Then the Deer Mothers lead the procession back across the snow into the mountains, while all those present at the Deer Dance are impregnated with the invisible mystery of their own existence. Martiniano watches in a trance of terror, resisting for a while the irrational force of the ritual until, sensing the living truth of this ancient blood-drama, he feels renewed and drawn into life's pulsing miracle.

Awakened by the Deer Dance, Martiniano comes to realize that the live deer in the mountains that ran to Flowers Playing, the deer enacted in the ritual, and even the deer he killed are all one in spirit, the embodiment of primordial forces that humans must seek to understand. The members of the pueblo know that the Deer Dance has been handed down from the tribe's beginnings, and that the deer embodies the grace of spirit that transcends them and is at the center of their origins. They know that with the first breath of life, each sentient being partakes of the cosmic breath through which it enters physical existence and the life of the spirit, that it is a different reflection yet an intimate part of the greater invisible whole. Martiniano also understands this ancient truth through Flowers Playing's pregnancy. During her pregnancy and when she gives birth, he sees her as a transpersonal part of Mother Earth's regenerative and creative capacity. After the baby's birth, when she becomes again the wife he knows, Martiniano gives her the deerskin hanging on the wall—the skin of the deer he killed—to make moccasins for their new son.

Now a father, Martiniano must choose which way of life he wants for his son—the comfortable, material life of the white man or the inward life of the pueblo people, including their outward appearance of poverty. He decides to run in the pueblo's annual ritual race, which symbolizes meeting the wonder of creation that will sustain the tribe for the new year and represents facing the personal and universal limits of flesh. He feels at one with the others who are running the race for themselves as well as for all humanity. The sense of wonder he feels from his son's birth, from the Deer Dance, and from running in the race helps Martiniano find and accept the faith for which he has been searching. There is no preordained secure road, he realizes. Faith requires the courage to jump into the dark and endure the journey, as the deer leaps into the night forest. He sees that all peoples must face the paradox of fleeting flesh and abiding spirit; the many faiths of different peoples are all attempts to live with this universal mystery.

The deer that he killed no longer haunts Martiniano. He joins with the life of his people. As he watches a Round Dance circle around the fire and listens to his people sing, he looks up at the sky one night and sees the great constellation of the Deer: the stars form the legs, the uplifted tail, the five-pointed antlers, and the markings on the body of one great deer—the Deer that is *all* deer, including the deer that he killed. If one looks long enough, far enough, high enough, and deep enough, he realizes, nothing is killed or lost. All beings can be found transmuted in another form, just as he now sees the bold pattern of the deer he killed twinkling brightly in the night sky, showing its transcendence to all who care to raise their eyes to see it.

Martiniano's spiritual journey differs in outward form from Jody's in *The Yearling,* and from that of the mythic hunter

Placidus. Yet the deer as spirit guide leads each person inwardly to the same overwhelming truth. Spiritual growth requires sacrifice of the lesser for the greater and acceptance of the death of a limited identity for a self that can relate to all of life. Martiniano learns that by killing the deer without respect, he alienated himself from his people. The man who kills the deer with disrespect wounds his own faith and wonder at existence. As he learns to confront and honor the spirit of the deer he killed, Martiniano feels reverence for the whole of life and especially for the feminine force of creation. He discovers the truths of the pueblo people: that all are children living through the grace of Mother Earth; that existence requires one life to give way to another; that the sacrificed life continues through conscious reverence in rituals like the Deer Dance or in wearing the moccasins made of the deer's sacred skin.

This is the lesson Jody learns when he sacrifices the yearling for his family's survival. Through sacrificing the deer, he not only marks the passage from boyhood to adult life, but moves from bitterness to faith by accepting the necessity of sacrifice in the paradox of survival. Also paradoxically, he sees that through his love of the deer he has become a responsible member of his earthly family, yet he can continue to be one with his spirit guide in that "other world" beyond ordinary physical, waking life.

In contrast to Martiniano and Jody, the hunter Placidus learns the miracle of transformation by saving the life of the deer and bowing down in humility and awe before the stag that becomes the Christ. For Placidus, salvation comes through compassion and sparing the life of another being; in *The Yearling* salvation comes through necessary sacrifice; and in *The Man Who Killed the Deer* salvation comes through a resurrection of dead spirits—both the soul of Martiniano and of the deer and Nature. The different tasks in each of the tales show the paradox of existence and the importance of distinguishing an appropriate choice and action from inappropriate ones.

Whatever the way, the deer represents an interior and exterior spiritual power, one that demands reverence and that in return can guide our lives.

Five

THE JOURNEY
BETWEEN LIFE
AND DEATH

n an ancient legend of the Sami people, a pair of great antlered reindeer—a doe and a bull—pull the sun each day across the sky to the four corners of the cosmos. The Sami word for *rein,* from which the word *reindeer* is derived, means the "way" to the four cosmic corners.[1]

The divine antlered couple drawing the great golden sun chariot across the heavens is a striking image for the sacred marriage of our interior masculine and feminine qualities, as well as for the spiritual journey on which humans must consciously embark to join these opposites within their own lives and psyches. The celestial journey of the reindeer couple as well as the birthing journey of the earthly reindeer can also be seen as a metaphor for men and women on the way to the wedding, on the path to the divine union of the yin and yang energies of the Tao. This sacred marriage can be embodied in three spheres: the interior wedding of masculine and feminine within a human being, the soul-mate wedding of lovers, and the cosmic wedding of heaven and earth, which engenders the mystical journey between life and death for all of us.

When I began my quest to discover why the reindeer image touched my soul so deeply, I did not know that reindeer migrate every year to give birth. Nor did I know that the shamanic peoples of the Arctic view the reindeer as a spirit guide that will help them make the final earthly passage through death by carrying their souls to the Other World. I knew only that the enigmatic reindeer called to me persistently, as if they were trying to lead me somewhere. So I began to study their habits and lore.

Every spring, when the ice and snow start melting in the Arctic, thousands of pregnant reindeer and caribou begin running north toward the high mountain valleys where they were born, leading the males and young ones with them. In the vast silence of the Arctic, the grunting sounds of reindeer mothers calling to their yearlings and the clicking, clacking sounds of hooves and tendons by which they alert one another to danger from predators creates an eerie music of excitement and urgency. Usually led by an elder pregnant doe, they travel hundreds of miles across the Arctic tundra over ice, snow, marsh, mud, and perilous permafrost. They forge river torrents, brave polar winds, and outrun wolf packs and other predators—facing death to give birth to the next generation.

Their physical journey can be seen as a symbol for the spiritual migration of human beings searching for the meaning of life in the everyday world. Our spiritual journeys, too, take us through bogs of unconsciousness. We too must pass through raging rivers of grief, tread carefully over areas of icy despair, cross craggy ravines that reflect our terror of the unknown, and face feared enemies that threaten to devour us, like hungry wolf packs. As the earthly reindeer struggles to dig up grass and lichen for food to fuel her journey, so we must strive to find what nurtures our spirit. The reindeer's ability to survive on their annual migration provides a metaphor for the way humans can endure on the creative quest for individual meaning for themselves and for future generations.

The tundra, across which the reindeer run, is like the uneven terrain of interior life that the soul must traverse. The Arctic's low-lying rainbow-hued vegetation is splashed on the sides of mountains and in valleys like a multicolored, layered spongy carpet, which can grow in areas where short summers impede the growth of trees. Beneath the tundra floor covering, the ground is permanently frozen. Because permafrost hinders drainage, the ground stays waterlogged during the summer thaw, making travel difficult. Travelers across the tundra feel the soft and springy turf under their feet and hear the squishy, crunchy vibrations of frozen tufts as they negotiate the uncertain, slippery, muddy bogs. As they walk across the unstable tundra, knowing that there is ice deep beneath the ground brings to their imagination the mystery of how life springs up from water. The wanderer crossing the changing tundra confronts human finitude through the challenge of surviving nature's physical wilds as well as the interior wilderness of the soul.

The reindeer's movements follow the seasons, just as the human soul must learn to move with the cyclical orbits of earthly life. The reindeer's capacity to move through treacherous terrain in different seasons corresponds to the adaptability that humans need to travel through our interior landscapes and weather its seasons. In winter, reindeer must wander incessantly in the Arctic's dark nights, always in search of lichen, a high-energy food buried in the snow that provides a reserve of fat that helps the deer endure the extreme polar winter so that they can make their springtime journey to give birth.

Like the reindeer, we, too, must learn to endure the coldest and darkest times of difficulty and suffering in our lives, and to store up spiritual food, or faith, so we can survive hard times. Transforming hopelessness into faith requires digging into the depths of the soul, just as the reindeer must dig deep in the snow for lichen. The passage for humans from winter into spring is difficult, as attested to by the high incidence of suicides in springtime and can be considered similar to the journey reindeer must make through the treacherous ice floes to the fawning grounds. This transit from dormancy to rebirth can be a most troublesome crossing. We must learn to surrender a desperation to which we sometimes become attached through the bitter pride of resentment. We need to relinquish torment in order to acknowledge and be open to the hope conveyed by the bright buds and green shoots that sprout in spring. As T. S. Eliot expressed it in his poem *The Waste Land:* "April is the cruellest month . . ."[2] In transition, we must come to terms with the pain and accept the ordeal of inner Dark Nights and the interior wasteland; then we must let go of bitterness so we can rejoice in the blooming of our new selves.

In his long poetic lament, *The Duino Elegies,* Rainer Maria Rilke expressed the excruciating despair humans feel once they have awakened to the limitations inherent in the human condition. After years of emotional struggle, Rilke surrendered to the fact that human lives like animals' move cyclically with nature. Rilke affirmed that despite the sufferings that life brings up, even *one* spring was so beautiful that he could commit to the whole of life.

To continue the seasonal metaphor, in summer the reindeer enjoy the warmth of the sun and the company of their young as they graze on the plentiful foliage, just as the summer of human life gives us the opportunity to enjoy a fullness of accomplishment and maturity of relationship. But reindeer are also forced to move continually to escape the mosquitoes and black flies that plague them; they do not expect to find an "endless summer" or permanent idyll. The mosquitoes and black flies suggest the psyche's "gadflies" that prod humans to keep growing rather than settle into easy but stagnant solutions.

In autumn, reindeer return with their young to the lower woodlands, where they eat cloud berries, cranberries, and blueberries as well as fungi, birch, juniper, sedges, scrub willow, and other plants, trees, and grasses of the tundra. Just as the reindeer enjoy a natural fall plenitude, so in the autumn of human lives we can reap the harvest of our own maturation to be ready for the next winter.

The reindeer's physical makeup also has interesting aspects and analogies to the human condition. For instance, reindeer have special cleft hooves for running across the tundra. Their hooves spread to support them on the soft ground in summer and on the snow in winter; they have sharp edges that give them stability on the ice. With these expandable hooves, reindeer can navigate over sedge tussocks, grassy clumps rounded on the tops and narrow at the base.

Just above the hoof the reindeer has an extra set of

"hooves" called dew claws. On soft ground, the dew hooves spread out, affording even greater surface area to the already spreading cleft hoof, giving the reindeer four natural snow-shoes with which to run over deep snow fields, icy ground, and boggy marshes that are impassable for humans. These hooves also help them swim well and are good for digging through the deep snow for food for as long as ten hours a day.[3]

The reindeer's spreading hooves and dew claws are comparable to the different stances, standpoints, and grounding by which humans adjust to different conditions along life's way. The dew claws may be analogous to our ancient instincts to adapt in order to survive. We learn to ground ourselves on the soul's journey to find meaning in life, we learn to have traction and stability when faced with life's torrents and abysses. During our interior winters, we learn how to tread confidently the slippery, frozen places of despair without denying or anesthetizing our emotions, and we learn to immerse ourselves in the deep waters of depression without drowning.

"Queens of the tundra," the poet Marianne Moore once called the reindeer mothers that run across the Arctic plains wearing their antlered crowns. Among reindeer, females are the favored survivors. By late autumn, most of the mature females are pregnant, and they have kept their antlers longer than the males' so they can defend themselves from bulls in the competition for food. When winter comes, the males tend to be weaker than the females due to the earlier loss of their antlers and because they have expended so much energy during the rutting season.

Pregnant reindeer carry their young about seven and a half months and usually give birth between May and mid-June.

Within a day or two of its birth, the calf can run along with its mother. It is weaned by late autumn. Nevertheless, it stays with its mother through the winter and into the following spring since it depends on the mother to dig food.

The reindeer's lives are arduous. They have adapted to the severe Arctic environment and are the only big mammals that can sustain themselves in large numbers on the tundra. On their annual migration to the calving grounds, the herd streams across the tundra with mysterious energy. Nothing can stop them. They can run for long distances at a speed of twenty-five miles an hour. The bulls are often far behind the does.

The weaker animals can be injured or die during the treacherous icy river crossings. The deer are also preyed upon by wolves, although a reindeer mother can protect herself and her young with her antlers and often turns away the attacker. Once the deer arrive at their calving grounds, they are relatively safe from predators and can find their food plants more readily. The herds stay in the mountains until late summer, when they return south to take refuge in the taiga, the dwarfed evergreen forests of Siberia, Eurasia, and North America.

In winter, the reindeer's fur coats allow them to survive at temperatures below minus 76 degrees Fahrenheit. The hair of their coats can be two inches thick, and the individual follicles are hollow and trap warmed air around the deer. The trapped air in the hollow follicles gives the reindeer buoyancy when they swim across rivers.[4]

The reindeer's hollow hair provides an image for the psychological adaptation humans need to make. We need to warm and wrap a protective insulation around us when we fall into the abysmal cold waters of extreme emotional conditions and dark wintry periods. At such times, we need to be buoyed, without drowning, in our "night sea journeys" toward transformation. We need to have faith that we can survive the blasts of inner blizzards and to find our own natural, warm, animating energies to help us survive barren, desolate times and conditions. Just such a process is depicted in the following story of Katerina.

A Czechoslovakian woman, Katerina, still living in her native country, came up to me in tears after I had presented a lecture, "The Reindeer Woman in the World's Dark Night," at an international conference in Prague. Throughout her life, Katerina had had recurring dreams and waking images in which she rode a reindeer to free herself from the confines of an oppressive government. Growing up during the Communist regime, Katerina felt trapped in her country. To escape the rigid Soviet domination that prohibited people from traveling and that condemned religious practice, Katerina would imagine she was riding a reindeer in Lapland, which all her life she wanted to do.

When Katerina was a little girl, her mother had comforted her by reading her fairy tales, in a number of which a reindeer had helped a heroine to freedom. In particular, Katerina remembered "The Snow Queen," a fairy tale by Hans Christian Andersen. In it, the heroine, Gerda, rides a reindeer in search of the realm of the frightening Snow Queen who has bewitched and imprisoned her boyfriend, Kay. The Snow Queen has frozen his heart and obscured his vision with a shard of ice. Before entering the Snow Queen's domain, the reindeer carries Gerda to two old women who mother her. One old woman nurtures Gerda physically with food, drink, and shelter, while the other nourishes her spiritually by letting her know that she has within herself the power to face the fearsome Snow Queen. With the reindeer's help, Gerda reaches the land of the Snow Queen, finds Kay, and cries as she runs to hug him. As Gerda embraces him, her warm tears fall on his frozen heart and melt it and clear his vision, breaking the Snow Queen's spell.

To the adult Katerina, the Snow Queen represented the freezing Soviet forces that had bewitched her country, while Gerda's and her own power lay in their open, loving nature. The imprisoned Kay was a symbol of Katerina's inner masculine energies held hostage by the Soviet system; the reindeer, a spirit guide that helped Gerda—and would help Katerina—make the journey to freedom. Remembering the image of Gerda riding the reindeer to free the captive boy helped Katerina to maintain her spiritual freedom and integrity.

When Katerina learned that female reindeer have antlers that they can use to protect themselves and their young, she cried with tears of joy and release. She told me she felt that all of these years, she had been using her inner reindeer antlers to protect the freedom of her soul. Learning that her inner image of the antlered female reindeer's power to defend herself was in accordance with outer fact helped confirm her enormous inner effort to protect herself and maintain spiritual freedom while captive in a totalitarian country.

Like Katerina and Gerda, we must trust our heart to launch us on a spiritual journey appropriate for us. The heart can lead us anywhere—to walk in the wilderness or to pray in an empty cathedral. Such moments can urge us to explore personal childhood memories, or inspire us to listen to a symphony through which we feel the human spirit. It may also lead us to direct contact with life that we've never before experienced: to walk in the streets of a city like Calcutta and help the poor or to be moved by injustice to participate in a political rally.

Our spiritual journeys ask us to be quiet and attentive in the face of mystery and to open ourselves to the unexpected, to become aware of the spirit guides all around us. Wherever we are—at home, outdoors in the streets, or even in the confined space of a prison, like the Bird Man of Alcatraz—if we are open and attentive, we may be visited by a spirit guide who will lead us to internal and external places that can change our lives—places that we never dared to dream that we could find. Spirit guides may appear to us in dreams, or even in reveries. Trust your heart, and it will lead you to find meaning within all the perplexing passages of existence, especially in the passage between birth and death.

In shamanic cultures, reindeer are tantamount to angels who can travel back and forth between heaven and earth, messengers of the spirit world. Just as earthly reindeer make a physically demanding journey to give birth, in the shamanic world they conduct the shaman along the arduous route to the spirit world, from which he brings back healing for the community. The reindeer make this trip again whenever a person dies—transporting the human soul for which they are responsible to the transcendent realm. In this way reindeer can be seen to represent a kind of archetypal guide for our earthly passage toward death.

As I wrote this chapter, my own life journey demanded that I accept the paradox of life and death. While in the midst of writing, my mother suddenly became ill. Her illness was diagnosed as terminal, and synchronistically, for the first time in my writing career, I found I could not write.

In despair about my mother's illness, I also began to lose hope that I would ever write again. I was faced with anxiety, pain, and death—that of my mother and of my own future as a writer. I wanted to escape from the torment of these worries and return to the mystical state and ecstatic passion that the reindeer had evoked in me. I was deeply afraid that I had lost my connection to this precious feeling.

While I was in this anguish, seeing that I had done all I could for my mother at that point in her illness, I had the opportunity to participate in a sweat lodge led by a Lakota woman and her son in the Rocky Mountains near Winter Park, where thirty of us would build the lodge for the ceremony by ourselves. After we had located the appropriate aspens, we asked their permission to use them for our ritual, and we sprinkled them with tobacco, considered a sacred offering by the Lakotas. Then, praying to the four directions, the sky, and the earth, we cut and gathered the aspen tree trunks and branches from the forest. We dug holes in the ground to plant the poles, then tied them together with colored ribbons: black for the west, red for the north, yellow for the east, white for the south, green for the earth, and blue for the heavens. The door built in the east–west direction was for the spirits, while the north–south direction represented the red road that is the human path.

Each of us purified ourselves in a smudging ceremony, and then we entered the sweat lodge on our knees from the east. We squatted in a circle, huddling to the ground. Water was poured onto the smoldering stones in the center arc; the steaming water vapors rose around us, filling the thick air with the scent of smoking rocks and sage. The Lakota led us in prayer, in which we were invited to open ourselves to receive the healing available from the four directions. As we crouched and crowded together, we felt the earth's grit on our skin, the steam mixed with drops of our common perspiration, and we were grateful for the air that bound us together, the breath of the spirit through which we have life. We were one. There was no space for inflated images of ourselves, no leeway for ego, no margin for false pride.

Humbly, each of us asked for direction. I prayed for healing for my mother, for a good passage for her to the next world if that was to be, and for spiritual healing for myself. Bitterness about life's injustices had invaded my heart during this time of despair, and I prayed for its removal so that I could be open to receive a new vision of life and the ability to write again. Toxins that had collected in my body were released through drops of perspiration. Eventually, I experienced a sudden sense of expansion and ecstasy. I heard the stones in the center singing. I felt free. I had turned my will over to the greater forces.

As we crawled out of the sweat lodge, I felt open and unburdened, serene and spiritually renewed. Later, I learned that the structure of the sweat lodge is patterned on the female rib cage, or the primal shape of an archetypal mother. I also learned that the sweat lodge is considered a purification ceremony and a rebirthing ritual in which the participants return to the womb and are reborn. Antlers are also sometimes placed next to the altar at the entrance of a sweat lodge to protect the spirit gate and to prevent evil from entering into this holy realm.

The next day, I went cross-country skiing in one of those sudden sparkling late spring snows that happen high in the Rocky Mountains. The invigoration and bliss of moving across the snow reminded me once more of the Sami people, who follow the reindeer on cross-country skis in winter. The rapture of cross-country skiing was mixed with the continuing feeling of purification of the sweat lodge, so that my awareness was heightened, ecstatic, and inspired. Later, at

Mount Princeton hot springs, I bathed in the natural steaming waters from the earth, which continued the deep feeling of baptismal blessing that I had received from the sweat lodge.

That night, I dreamed that hundreds of black-and-white spotted wild horses, along with their foals, were running past me through an entryway. Overwhelmed by their beauty, I ran after them to watch them as long as I could. I saw one filly returning, so I ran toward it, hugged it, and picked her up to take her home. I knew she had come back to entrust herself to me.

The energy of the wild horses in the dream promised a return of energy, one that needed loving care. It showed that an entryway that had been barred—my writer's block and stored resentment—was now open, wide enough indeed for hundreds of mother horses to run through with their newborn foals. I felt they related to Dolly, my first spirit guide, to the reindeer spirit, and to the deep mystery of a mother's birth-giving.

A few days later another dream followed—one that finally broke through my despair and my writer's block. In the dream I was in a large mountain meadow, where a national Jungian conference was in process. It was announced that I would give a spontaneous presentation on the Reindeer Woman that evening. I wondered why I had been asked to talk on this theme and doubted that the participants would be able to relate to the reindeer motif. Suddenly I heard the sound of rumbling hooves and felt the reverberating ground. Turning around, I saw thousands of reindeer running toward the meadow. For a moment I seemed to be above them, and I glimpsed an aerial view of their antlers—a spectacle of nature's cathedral spires rising from the reindeer's heads and crossing the earth. Then the reindeer were with me in the meadow, just as they had been present in reality in Siberia. How could anyone, I wondered in the dream, not be in awe of this miracle?

The reindeer glowed with supernatural beauty. They entered a huge corral and one by one were marked, then left to return to wherever they'd come from. When the last reindeer had gone, I realized it was time to begin my talk. My own analyst, who in real life had written a book about shamanism, was standing there beaming, about to introduce me. I now understood why I had been chosen to give this presentation —it was part of an initiation.

This dream filled me with joy and hope and rekindled the inspiration I had felt in Siberia. I knew that the reindeer had come running to me in my dream to remind me of my mission—to write about them and their gift of beauty and to tell about the meaning that they bring to humans. Reflecting on the dream, the marking of the reindeer in the corral meant that they received the brand of human consciousness, which would make their way of life comprehensible and significant to human life.

The poet Rilke thought that the invisible energies of the cosmos actually want to be made visible and discernible in the consciousness of humankind so that they can be embodied in human life. It seemed to me that through my dream, the reindeer spirit had announced its overwhelming desire to be heard and understood in this world. I wanted to become a conscious channel through which the reindeer could communicate their spiritual essence.

The dream reindeer that had come of their own accord into the corral suggested to me that their energy could be held (corralled) so that I could write about them, and so that they could be spiritually incarnated in return. I wondered if the branding of the reindeer reflected my calling to write this book. The image of the reindeer leaving the corral freely, one by one, seemed like an image of the way words come out in telling a story. The talk that I was to give seemed like an opportunity to impart spiritual significance. The small opening through which the reindeer entered and left the corral reminded me of the small opening through which I had crawled in and out of the sweat lodge, where I had been spiritually stamped. The dream seemed to mark my entry back into the world as a messenger to convey the reindeer's worth and beauty and to ground their magnificence.

On a personal level, I felt that the dream reindeer had announced the birth of a new child—the reindeer book— and carried it to me via dream life, cradling the newborn creative vision in their antlers. Ironically, just as my mother was dying, I was giving birth in another form. The deep bond between my mother and myself that I had felt so strongly as a child, then seemingly had lost during adolescence, and later began to reforge as we both matured together, seemed somehow connected with the bond to my creative child, the reindeer book. The awareness that death and birth were happening side by side was painful and enigmatic, and it haunted me. Then quite suddenly, my mother died. I was unable to get to her bedside to be with her in her last moments.

My mother's death threw me anew into the abyss of suffering. For a long time I woke up in the mornings crying. The loss of my mother caused me to feel homeless, abandoned like an orphan. In dream after dream I was trying to find my home. The houses I searched for were always faulty. Someone or something was always missing, and sometimes the houses were dangerous. In one dream I was back in my mother's house, but the entire front wall fell down.

Once more I was plunged into a new cycle of the Soul's Dark Night, into the paradox of good and evil. It seemed unjust to me that my mother had died so painfully from lung cancer when she had never smoked. Before she died, my mother told me from the hospital that despite her pain and exhaustion, she was fighting hard to survive so that she could return home. She never had that chance.

I began to question anew the enigmas of injustice, suffering, and pain. I began to doubt that there really was life after death, rebirth, or immortality. Like Ivan Karamazov, and Job before him, I asked why a creator would heartlessly allow the innocent to suffer.

Then I had another dream in which I was invited to travel by marine ferry at night with a group of women. The scene changed, and I was in a city and had to make my way through a tough neighborhood past a gang of dangerous teenage boys. The neighborhood was similar to the one in which I had grown up. Collecting my courage, I passed by the gang without harm and turned a corner. There to my right was the house of my childhood. It had been converted into a national heritage monument in honor of the only surviving member of its species—a huge shiny, silver lizard that sat on a rock.

As I looked in amazement at the luminous lizard, a creature that I realized belonged to two worlds—the earthly and the supernatural realms—I saw that it was my mother in a new form. I woke up feeling that I had been given a glimpse of the alchemical process of transformation and that my mother had sent a message to me from the other world in the form of this dream.

This dream was clearly related to a strange experience I had had in waking life. I was walking in the woods and came upon a lizard and snake in a life and death struggle. After nearly half an hour, the snake managed to swallow the lizard, then slithered its swollen body into the dark recesses of some blackened logs.

Looking up, I saw graying storm clouds gather in the sky, casting shadows on the earth. I fell into a gloomy, foreboding mood and had a premonition that my mother's condition had changed unexpectedly. Just a few hours earlier, her nurse had told me that she was sleeping, and she suggested that I call later so that I would not disturb her.

I rushed back from my hike to find a telephone. When I called the hospital, I was informed that she was dead.

I associated the silver lizard in the dream with the actual lizard I had seen at the time of my mother's death, as well as with the lizards that ancient alchemists kept with them during their work to transform base matter into gold—a metaphor for the work that humans must undertake as they transform their lives. Later, I learned that some Native American people associate the lizard with dream vision and consider the snake to be the underworld serpent of wisdom and power, and the ally and helping friend of the deer, bearer of the spirit of grace.

While grieving over the illness and death of my mother, I felt I had lost the reindeer spirit once again. The writer's block returned. Where had the reindeer and their spirit gone—those hundreds of reindeer that had come, unforeseen, down from the misty mountain toward me? I thought again of how they left one by one after being marked by an invisible force and returned in the direction from whence they had come. Amidst my grief, my musings on the sudden coming and going of the dream reindeer reminded me of the following ancient Eskimo tale:[5]

The reindeer on which the people of a certain village depended had disappeared. The reindeer regularly journeyed to a region within the Inland Ice, the villagers knew, but no one had ever dared to travel there. The dangers of this journey included passing by the threatening Dog-Headed People and the Thrashing Spirits. So the people asked a shaman to see if he could find out where the reindeer had gone. After the shaman went into a trance, he communicated with his spirit guide, who told him about the House of Reindeer. Led by the spirit guide, the shaman traveled for two full moons to the place of the Inland Ice.

The journey was arduous, but his guide helped him keep warm by mending his boots and pants, and since the shaman could make himself invisible, he was not attacked by the Dog-Headed People or the Thrashing Spirits. After a long time the guide said, "When we stop here at dusk, you will see the House of Reindeer. But if you kill even one of them or have the wish to do so, you will be transformed into the lowest creature on earth."

When twilight came, the shaman discovered that he was standing beside a tremendous ice-house. Nearby, he saw a herd of reindeer grazing. After each reindeer had finished eating, it went into the house. All through the night the shaman stayed there watching, but the flow of reindeer heading into the house never seemed to end. The sight of the reindeer streaming into the ice-house was the most beautiful he had ever witnessed. Finally the shaman returned home. When the people asked him about his journey, he could not risk telling them about the wondrous place he had seen, for he feared that they would travel there themselves and kill all the beautiful reindeer. That was how the story ended.

Perhaps the elusive reindeer, I mused, disappeared into their mysterious home to draw each of us to journey to see their eternal loveliness, and to learn that we can appreciate their splendor only when we cease to want to kill and own them. Perhaps the icy despair and doubt that prevented me from continuing on my own journey was my desire to have things go the way I thought they should be and to hold on to people and places in order to possess them. Perhaps the place where my mother had gone was the mysterious ice-house, where now she could finally see the reindeer and glory in their beauty.

Shortly before my mother died, she had confided in me a waking vision that disturbed her because she could not quite comprehend it. She was being prepared to go somewhere on a long journey, she said, and she was afraid she was never coming back. Someone had taken all her old clothes. All around her, people were celebrating. Their voices sounded different and strange. She suspected that they were preparing a special party for her since she had overheard that they were planning to give her a beautiful rose-colored dress for a surprise event.

My mother had actually requested in her will that she be dressed for her funeral in a rose gown. I was reminded of Rilke's request that a verse about the rose, symbol of the great mystery, be inscribed upon his gravestone, and I turned to his great poetic cycle, *The Duino Elegies.* In it, he envisions death as the ultimate transformation and the threshold that affirms life, as Rilke himself wrote in a letter:

> *Affirmation of life-AND-death appears as one in the "Elegies."* To grant one without the other is, so it is here learned and celebrated, a limitation which in the end shuts out all that is infinite. *Death is* the *side of life* averted from us, unshone upon by us: we must try to achieve the greatest consciousness of our existence which is at

home in *both unbounded realms, inexhaustibly nourished from both. . . .* The true figure of life extends through *both* spheres, the blood of the mightiest circulation flows through *both: there is neither a here nor a beyond, but the great unity* in which the beings that surpass us, the "angels," are at home.[6]

Rilke's vision and the following poem, "How the Old Woman Met Death," by Mary Elizabeth Williams illustrate for me the spiritual journey we must learn consciously to accept on the passage from our first breath to our last at death.

> I'm invited to the reindeer dance;
> The tundra is their ballroom floor.
> We will glide and we will prance
> and our spirits will upwards soar.
> They will wear velvet suits and gowns;
> I, a kuspik of blue.
> We'll dance from sunset until dawn
> when the sky turns a golden hue.
> I am an old Yupik woman;
> They know I am their friend.
> We share a bond as old as time—
> One that will never end.
> They go dancing Northward
> As they've promises to keep.
> I lie down 'neath a grassy quilt
> To sleep the ancient sleep.[7]

Six

ANTLERS

hen reindeer run across the Arctic tundra, their antlers form a shifting, flowing image that resembles a great wave moving across the earth. Like great natural mobiles combining form and function, the antlers rattle as the reindeer run long distances across the open country. This strange sound, combined with the thunder of their hooves pounding the tundra, their grunting and barking calls to each other, and the eerie music of the Arctic wind, produce uncanny tones of a natural symphony.

The great sea of antlers is hypnotizing. The antlers' shape suggests spiritual antennae reaching to the sky, pointing to the spirit world, receiving messages and bearing the instinctive wisdom of death and rebirth. Antlers suggest the baton of a creative conductor directing a great symphony, the magic wand of a sorcerer, the divining rod of a visionary, or the drumstick of a shaman in ritual trance. It is easy to imagine antlers as supernatural lightning rods conducting vibrating electric energy from the heavens—energy that can bring creative rebirth and spiritual revelation as well as life and death.

The antlers' contour is formed by long spikes that curve to shape a cup, or arms uplifted to receive and hold an infant. Viewed from above, antlers appear to be cradles ready to carry the coming child, the embodiment of divine birth. No wonder that in human imagination the reindeer are honored creatures at the winter solstice and have been linked with Christmas.

Antlers suggest renewal of the self. The casting and regrowing of the reindeer's deciduous antlers require surrender to a greater natural force, just as at times we must relinquish outmoded ways we have adapted to life in order to enable our self-renewal. To ancient native peoples they represented the seed of new life and were used by women healers. Some tribes, like the Yolaikia, thought antlers were originally gifts to the deer from women, and many women have deer as part of their given names.

Just as actual antlers are shed every year and then grow again, following the cycle of death, rebirth, and renewal, so a dream of antlers can lead the dreamer to comprehend the need for personal spiritual regeneration. A woman in one of my workshops, Jill, dreamed of white antlers that emerged from newly tilled earth. She said that this dream came to her after she had told a therapist that she was feeling desperate. Her feeling was so extreme that she knew she was suffering from a spiritual deprivation. Her depression and lack of vitality were comparable to the stage in antler growth when the antlers have been shed and only small stumps are left. The dream of antlers spurred Jill to renew her spiritual practice. She searched for and found a set of antlers, which she placed on a table where she kept ritual objects. The antlers became part of an altar where she could worship in her own way, just as the Sami people of old worshipped at sacred sites where they built altars from antlers and stones. The dream of the antlers enabled Jill to recognize her budding spirituality and acknowledge her own mystical nature.

The reindeer's antlers are considered by some to cradle the third eye, that special, inherent form of intuitive knowledge. The third eye can guide us through difficult times to higher knowledge. Toni, who attended a workshop in the Northeast, related a dream in which she was resting, cradled up high in the antlers of a reindeer. She didn't know how to get back down to the ground or, if she made it, how to come again to the safety of the antlered cradle. She noticed, in the dream, that her therapist was standing nearby, whereupon she realized that her therapist could help her learn how to make the passage back and forth between the ground and the secure cradle. In the nurturing cradle of the antlers, she knew, she would receive the vision that she needed in order to live purposefully, but she needed to embody her spiritual vision in everyday practical life as well. As a person afflicted with black depressions, resulting from seasonal affective disorder, she was inspired by the reindeer's ability to survive in the dark night.

Like the branching of antlers, intuition branches out in many directions and is sensitive to heart vibrations, creative urges, and inspiration. Antlers are like a divining rod for spiritual knowledge, a resting place for vision, and a bridge to imagination. Antlers remind me of times in the creative process when we must rest, patient and still, while the creative impulse is forming, as if we were waiting in the woods to allow a deer to approach.

Creative intuitions can be as shy and elusive as a reindeer in the forest. Rilke felt that all spiritual growth requires walking the path of patience. The creative process, too, entails waiting until the best time to grow. To me, Rilke's description of spiritual and creative growth applies to the process of allowing the spiritual significance of the reindeer quest to emerge and echos the way the reindeer people live. The following words, which Rilke wrote to a young poet searching to find his way in life, vibrate like the branching antlers of the reindeer, transmitting the wisdom of the spirit-world:

> . . . all progress, must come from deep within and cannot be pressed or hurried by anything. *Everything* is gestation and then bringing forth. To let each impression and each germ of a feeling come to completion wholly in itself, in the dark, in the inexpressible, the unconscious, beyond the reach of one's own intelligence, and await with deep humility and patience the birth-hour of a new clarity: that alone is living the artist's life: in understanding as in creating. There is here no measuring with time, no year matters, and ten years are nothing. Being an artist means, not reckoning and counting, but ripening like the tree which does not force its sap and stands confident in the storms of spring without the fear that after them may come no summer. It does come. But it comes only to the patient, who are there as though eternity lay before them, so unconcernedly still and wide. I learn it daily, learn it with pain to which I am grateful: *patience* is everything![1]

Antlers are one of nature's most marvelous creations. Because of my own and other women's dreams of antlers, I became intrigued with their possible significance for our spiritual life. Since northern shamans don reindeer antlers to perform their spiritual rituals, perhaps antlers have an interior archetypal presence in our psyches.

Only animals in the deer family have antlers. In spring, the antlers begin to form from two permanent bone stumps, called pedicles, on the deer's head. While they are developing, the antlers are soft and tender and covered with velvet, a thin skin containing thousands of blood vessels that carry calcium and other minerals for building strong bones. Even though the antlers reach full size after three months, they remain covered with the velvet until the bone inside is hard. By late summer, when the antlers are established, they begin to shed the velvet, and the shiny new antlers can be seen.

As the velvet peels away, it often hangs in long bloody strips from the antlers, like crimson streamers announcing the annual parade of transformation. The bloody velvet is also reminiscent of menstrual blood, a sign of a woman's creative cycle and once a component of ancient shamanic ceremonies. The curve of the antlers, reminiscent of the moon, suggests the cosmic waxing and waning of feminine transformation connected with the moon's phases.

In winter, as the antlers become very hard near the skull, they fall off, leaving only the small stumps on the deer's forehead, which soon will be covered once more with velvet to allow the new and tender antlers to grow again. Shed antlers become weathered and, eventually, part of the soil. The minerals in the antlers provide nutrients for the plants the deer eat in order to grow new antlers in a natural recycling.[2]

The growth of antlers actually parallels our own inner

process of development. Just as antlers initially are soft and tender, we, too, are delicate and fragile in the rudiments of our developmental process. Similarly, a creative idea is tender in its beginnings, just as a fragile fetus is encased in a sack within the uterus inside the pregnant woman's body. Sometimes we adapt a hard persona, or outer appearance, in order to survive in society, and we suppress our tender feelings despite the fact that personal growth requires gentleness for humility and openness. Although we may cover up our tenderness or even try to suppress it altogether, because mistakenly we regard it as weak, it is this very tenderness that grounds our capacity for kindness and compassion and that allows us to be open and receptive.

The new tender antlers are like soft, tender little shoots of young plants, and like those sticky green leaves that bud in spring, they remind us every year that new life returns. In Dostoyevsky's *The Brothers Karamazov,* the skeptical brother, Ivan, cynically argues about the existence of God with his gentle brother, Alyosha, a compassionate young man who feels life's pain but also sees its beauty. Alyosha replies that there must be some greater divine forces that transcend us. While berating God for the suffering and injustices of this world, Ivan suddenly is overcome with an image of budding leaves, and he confesses to his brother that sometimes he too believes there is something greater. The tender antlers, like the first leaves of growth, offer us an image of hope.

The natural process of antler growth has a sensitive beginning and can remind us of our own delicate nature. The velvet covering that protects the antlers and contains the minerals for growth suggests the nourishing, safeguarding resources that we have within ourselves. Imagine touching the velvet of the antlers—how soft and smooth it would feel to your hand, as if you were wearing a velvet glove! The velvet covering, necessary for strengthening the bone, suggests the smooth and "velvet touch" of feminine gentleness, lush Eros that empowers us.

Sensitivity and softness are an inherent part of the antler cycle, and the antlers can remind us that at times in spiritual development, we must wait for strength. The velvet phase of antlers is an image that supports patience when we need to be gentle with ourselves or others. The way that antlers replenish themselves again and again, always relying upon the velvet for their growth at a certain stage in their development, suggests, for human evolution, a capacity for gentleness that is a source of potency, health, and endurance.

When it is time for the velvet to be shed from the antlers, the deer rub their antlers against trees and bushes so that the velvet will fall off and leave the pure, bare antlers. The covering that once was needed for protection would now inhibit the hardened antlers, so the antlers "itch" to have it removed. This happens in personal transformation, too, when we "itch" to show our strength and what we can accomplish in the world. Just as the reindeer rub off the velvet, so we need to hone our spirituality by scraping from our soul whatever we no longer need until we are left with the essential bones of our being. The end result—the strong, solid, shiny antlers—corresponds to our generative capacity to express and show off our beauty and vigor in creative works and in our own transforming lives.

An analogy that the Tibetan Buddhist teacher Chogyam Trungpa once offered about the development of the spiritual warrior is relevant here.[3] Trungpa compared the birth of the warrior to the first growth of a reindeer's antlers. In the beginning the antlers are so soft and tender, they seem too delicate to be of any help. At first, using them feels awkward. It is the same with the birth of the spiritual warrior, whose fearlessness comes from working with the subtlety of the human heart and who "fights" to embody compassion in everyday life. Fearlessness actually entails opening oneself and receiving. It means being strong enough to experience and be touched by our and others' underlying fears.

The tender heart is actually a strength that allows the spiritual warrior to extend herself. Just as the fully formed antlers stretch out to receive the vibrations in the air, the tender heart allows us to open to listening and talking meaningfully with others. The tender heart is compassionate; it can relate to itself and to all other beings with passion; it allows us to appreciate the world around us.

True fearlessness was the lesson that the protagonist of Peter Weir's film *Fearless* had to learn. After surviving an airplane crash, he felt no fear for the first time in his life. He began to test and express his fearlessness in superficial ways, becoming a reckless daredevil, tempting death by walking into oncoming traffic. Thinking that no one could understand what he had undergone, he also distanced himself from his wife and son. He was not beyond fear, of course, but in a kind of spiritual shock, he was defending himself against the trauma of his near death. He was also deflecting his sadness and vulnerability, and with it the wisdom to be gained from his experience.

Only by reaching out to another survivor, a woman whose child had died in the plane crash and who was in touch with her grief and vulnerability, was he able to open himself to love. Learning from her, he opened to his inner life and fears and started to paint the process of passing through the center of a spiral, similar to the passage that a shaman might make on the journey to the spirit world. He studied the mystical paintings of William Blake depicting the otherworldly journey. Finally he had a vision in which he was passing through the tunnellike hub of the plane that had crashed. Instead of going completely through the tunnel, he turned back—a symbol for reentering this world, just as the shaman may travel through a tunnel to the other world but returns to earth to share healing and wisdom with the community. His decision to live on earth in order to be with his wife and to teach his son what he had learned was the embodiment of his genuine fearlessness.

Reindeer antlers also point to the possibility of integrating the feminine and masculine. Their elongated, spiked antler beams are formed in a cuplike shape that contains both feminine and masculine images. It has even been hypothesized that young female reindeer and caribou have a relatively high level of androgens (male sex hormones) in their blood during the initial period of pedicle and antler development.

Female reindeer and their American cousins the caribou are unique because, unlike other female deer, they have antlers. Having antlers longer than the males enables the females to be as strong as the bulls during the winter when they must vie for the scarce food sources. They can use their antlers to dig down deep in the snow and scrape for the moss that both mother and calves eat, and also to push away the bigger bulls that have already lost their antlers. While the reindeer's first defense against predators is to run faster than its enemy the wolf, if necessary a reindeer mother can gore and injure a wolf that threatens her young and send this potential killer limping in retreat.

The antlers are a thrilling image for many women, who long for such strength and self-protective abilities that would also allow them to act out of the center of their tender, instinctive, feminine self. The image of self-protection and self-renewal offers hope for the possibility of a peaceful yet strong, inward and outward way of being that is an alternative to our culture's sharp, warlike manner. Women who are naturally gentle and have difficulty developing their aggressive side respond to the image of growing "psychic antlers" in order to protect their peaceful way.

Anne, a woman who was dealing with difficult family conflicts, remarked that learning about the reindeer's use of antlers as a way of protection provided her with an alternative to her tendency to butt into things like a ram with permanent horns, a habit that invariably hurt other people and herself. She needed an image for self-protection that didn't take the permanence of horns for granted but that could be strong, sharp, and protective when she needed it, and at other times soft or not there at all.

No wonder, then, that some women spontaneously paint self-portraits with antlers on their heads or dream about deer with antlers. When they look at the paintings or awake from the dream, they are puzzled, because they associate antlers with stags, yet in the dreams and the paintings the antlered figures feel feminine to them. The artists Georgia O'Keeffe and Frida Kahlo both painted antlers. Georgia O'Keeffe's dazzling paintings of both antlers and flowers express this archetypal feminine connection. Frida Kahlo's extraordinary self-portrait as an antlered deer with arrows piercing her bloody body presents the image of feminine wounding, an image I explore in Chapter 8, "The Wounded Deer."

Knowing that the reindeer doe has antlers can give a woman the feeling of freedom to be herself, unafraid of her own power. The reindeer doe adorned with her queenly crown of antlers, running to give birth, is a living embodiment of the power of the feminine principle. Upon hearing that female reindeer have antlers, Colleen, a woman who was searching for the sacred in her life, said that she had dreamed of a woman friend whose longtime commitment to embodying daily spiritual practice was an inspiration to her. In the dream Colleen was surprised to see that this woman was wearing antlers on her head. When her friend said to Colleen, "You have antlers too," this reaffirmed Colleen's spiritual commitment and linked it with her feminine creativity.

A dream of an antlered white reindeer leading the way marked the initiation for Marlene's transformation at the beginning of her therapy. In the dream, she was with a woman friend on the porch of her cabin in the woods. As her husband, who had been at the mailbox, turned to come back to the cabin, Marlene sensed a movement in the forest and motioned to him to be still. Suddenly, out from the woods came a white antlered reindeer that walked toward her left side. The white reindeer led other small deer and fawns, all part of a family or small herd, and moved slowly across the clearing to the left. Behind them followed other animals with their young in a parade across the clearing.

An initial dream at the beginning of therapy often reveals a major aspect of the psychological, emotional, and spiritual work that the dreamer needs to accomplish. This dream signaled the various animal energies that needed to emerge from the unconscious, symbolized by the forest, and that were approaching Marlene to be integrated into her conscious life. This movement of integration, central to the transformation process, was led by the antlered white reindeer, symbolizing the animal energy that was to blaze the way by directing her attention to the left, symbolic of the unconscious. A supernatural being to the Sami people of old, the white reindeer signifies the spiritual pathfinder that leads the way to integrating these animal energies.

• • •

Just as the reindeer's antlers suggest spiritual antennae and are worn by shamans in ritual journeys to the spirit world, so a dream of antlers can herald a visitation from another realm. Dana, an artist who was also on a spiritual search, dreamed of a sacred encounter with antlered animals from another sphere. In the dream Dana is trying to find the answer to a question that has been posed in a graduate psychology class. No one, not even experienced therapists, knows the answer. Knowing that the question is important, Dana decides to hike to a village where she has been told there lives a person who knows the answer. Going to the village entails hiking through a dense forest, a way that Dana follows until she comes to a clearing. There in a wide meadow she sees wild animals, all walking two by two. Two strange animals, their heads crowned with cariboulike antlers, approach her, walking upright on two stiltlike, stiff, furry legs. These extraordinary animals have long flat triangular bodies on which spirals and other primordial symbols are engraved.

As the antlered animals come toward her in the dream, Dana feels the sacredness of the encounter. She knows that she is meant to meet these antlered beings, which can shift their shape back into animals. The antlered animals come forward on their own—intuitive beings from another world. In the final scene of the dream, Dana reaches the village, where she goes into a luggage store. In the store, a friend offers to sell her an old heavy suitcase trimmed with leather and big floral designs. It has a garment bag of good quality attached. Although Dana needs only the garment bag, she thinks she can unzip it from the heavy suitcase. The dream ends with Dana trying to decide whether to purchase the bag.

The sacred encounter with the antlered beings from the other world was the focal point of the dream, Dana said. She knew that meeting the antlered animal couple was the genuine purpose of her quest. The "answer" to the question posed at school, Dana now understood, was in the quest itself rather than in theoretical explanations or practical solutions. For this journey led her to the hallowed meeting in the meadow, where surrounded by wild animal couples, she was invited by the antlered ones to embark in a new direction on her spiritual path. The image of the heavy suitcase in the last scene of the dream, Dana said, points to the extra baggage that we think we still need and that we tend to carry around with us even though we already have been shown our essential needs.

The spiritual energy of the dream of the white antlers and of the dream encounter with the antlered animals is a very real force, like the open-ended generativity of actual antlers as they emerge from the reindeer's head. The gift of antlers opens up the imaginal world, bringing us astonishing pictures, new words, innovative movements, surprising ideas, original impressions, and revolutionary thoughts.

When I remember my dream of the reindeer and the awesome view of their antlers, I am jolted from personal worries and from transitory fears, as though the antlers conducted lightning through their beams, communicating wisdom from a transpersonal realm. The image of antlers as revelatory receptors reminds me that inherent in our human nature is the potential to transform. Our capacity for consciousness, choice, and creative expression mark us to be the locus of revelation, the earthly beings through whom discovery takes place. If we are present every moment, we can open to receive the exciting images, sounds, movements, and words that bring us into contact with our spiritual and creative capabilities.

My physical journey to follow the reindeer and meet the Even people in Siberia manifested an essential aspect of the spiritual journey for us all—to bear in mind that transformation is possible even when we are faced with despair. Despite the horrendous conditions in Russia—the breakdown of the social system and economic organization, the malfunctioning communication and transportation systems, the desperation of individuals in the face of crumbling governmental law and order, the confusion of a deeply spiritual people who still value and care for the soul—somehow in the Arctic tundra, a people still live with integrity, their lives centered spiritually on the creative energy embodied in the reindeer.

Just as the reindeer running toward me in my dream stunned me with their beauty and transcendence and jarred me from the paralysis of my depression and writer's block, so the memory of the powers of regeneration that their antlers carry can shake me from compulsive thoughts and feelings that arrest my capacity to change. Whenever I am bogged down by personal worries, or larger concerns about the decline of our society, or the suffering of a country such as Russia, I try to recall the image of the running reindeer.

One gift that I received from my trip to the Siberian tundra is the realization that no matter how impossible things may seem, a hopeful symbol like the reindeer can help us go on living. Remembering that far away on the tundra reindeer run to give birth provides a sense of solace and healing. The image of thousands of reindeer running with their heads held high in dignity as their royal antlered crowns reach up toward the heavens can provide a divining rod that leads us to transcendence and offers a pure moment of beauty that can transport us from despair to joy and affirmation.

Seven

THE REINDEER
GODDESS

he ancient Arctic peoples honored the mysterious Reindeer Goddess—a supernatural being who roamed the polar mountains. Often depicted in animal rather than human form, the Reindeer Goddess's stately antlers sparkled, reflecting the northern lights; her hairy body held the mystery of the leafy taiga; and her hooves reflected the sun as they touched the earth and flew through the sky. She was the mother of all reindeer and was said to give birth to deer, sometimes to human children, and to the universe. Her gifts were bountiful. She watched over reindeer mothers giving birth and led them with their young to green grassy mountain pastures, where she protected them from harm so that they could graze freely. When it was time, in autumn, she led them back to the lower sheltered forests, where they were shielded from the harsh Arctic winds.

The Reindeer Goddess was worshipped by most of the peoples of the Arctic but was designated by different names. The Kola Sami people of Siberia prayed to a hairy reindeer goddess, the supernatural mistress of wild animals, calling her the Lady of the Reindeer or the Mistress of Wild Animals.[1] The Evenki people of Siberia called her Bugady, or Mother of the Universe. The Nganasan people of northern Asia believe, even now, that the mothering life-givers are pregnant deer whose bodies are covered with hair and whose heads sprout branching antlers.[2] For the Sami people of Lapland, the Reindeer Goddess is linked with the sun goddess, Beijenneite, who came to earth primarily in human form to remind the people, if they had forgotten, of the need for reverence for the reindeer and to teach them how to care for her cherished animals.[3] In Russia, as late as the twelfth century, the eastern Slavic people worshipped the reindeer divinity Rozhanitsa, the Mother Goddess of the North, at the winter solstice.[4]

All of these people felt the great mystery of the Reindeer Goddess and revered her through rituals. At the spring equinox they prayed to her for her guidance during the reindeer's great journey to give birth. At the summer solstice they honored her for her guardianship during the delivery of the baby reindeer and against beasts of prey. In autumn they thanked her for her safekeeping during the journey back to the lower lands, and in winter for her preservation of the reindeer during the long, harsh, freezing season.

In early times, the Sami people made great stone and antlered altars, called *seite,* which they placed in sacred sites,
usually along the ridges of rounded fells, the mountains fre-
quented by reindeer. The *seite* was a symbol for the original
deities of the ground that could provide good luck in hunting
reindeer. At the *seite,* they consecrated a chosen reindeer,
often a *vaja* or female reindeer, as their thankful offering to
the divinity, sacrificing one reindeer a year to the earth. To
honor the chosen animal, the reindeer was first adorned,
then slaughtered, then burned, then buried. The Sami people
also made an offering to the reindeer spirit at the first time in
the year that the reindeer were milked.[5]

The Paleolithic cave paintings of reindeer at Lascaux,
France, also show signs of homage, as do the female reindeer
skull and antlers mounted on a seven-foot ritual pole erected
at an ancient sacrificial site by the postglacial lake at
Stellmoor, Germany. Research has shown that the skull belonged to a sixteen-year-old reindeer doe, which accords
with the findings that old antlered does were the pathfinders
for the herd and were hallowed and consecrated by ancient
tribes.[6]

Later, the eastern Slavic people honored the Reindeer
Goddess at the winter solstice by embroidering her image in
red on white linen cloth. They baked cookies that they
frosted with white icing and formed in the shape of reindeer,
which they gave as presents for good luck. They offered
other bloodless sacrifices to her, such as bread, cheese, and
honey. This tradition was continued up to the early part of
the twentieth century, when the cookies and embroideries
were still offered at her feast.

Through the centuries, the Reindeer Goddess may well

have evolved into the Deer Goddess esteemed by the Gaelic and Celtic peoples. The Deer Goddess appears in fairy tales and legends, such as the Gaelic legend from the Finn Cycle *The Birth of Oisin*. This story tells of the beautiful maiden, Sadv. One day the Druid, Fir Doirch, (the "Black Man") sees Sadv and pursues her, but she repels his advances. Furious, the sorcerer transforms her into a deer, although one of his servants whispers to her that if she can get inside the fortress of Fiana, ruled by the king, Finn, she can regain her original form as a woman and the dark Druid will lose his power over her. Sadv roams the forests as a hind and is chased by many hunters, but she is so fast that none can catch her.

One day, when Finn is hunting with his men, he catches a glimpse of the fleet hind. Chasing the deer with his two trusty dogs, Finn is surprised when suddenly the deer lies down in a field and the dogs start to play with her, licking her face instead of attacking. Amazed, Finn takes the deer alive back to his home inside the fortress. During the night, Sadv appears to him in her original form as a beautiful woman and tells Finn about the spell that the Druid sorcerer has put upon her. Immediately, Finn falls in love with the beautiful Sadv, and the two live together joyfully. Sadv soon becomes pregnant with Finn's child.

Finn is outside the fortress one day when Sadv thinks she hears him call her. She goes out to meet him, but the one who called her name was not Finn but the Druid, Fir Doirch, in disguise. He changes her again into a hind. Sadv tries to run back into the fortress to safety, but the Druid's hounds catch her and drag her off into the forest. When Finn comes back and finds that Sadv is missing, he grieves for seven years and searches all over Ireland for the hind.

Although Finn cannot find Sadv, one day his dogs find a small boy in the woods and play with him, licking his face as they licked the deer earlier. Struck by the likeness between the boy and Sadv, Finn takes him home and raises him. As soon as the boy is old enough to talk, he tells Finn that he has been raised by a hind that was abducted by a dark man who touched the deer with a wand. When Finn hears this story, he realizes that the boy is Sadv's son, and he names him Oisin, which means "the fawn." When Oisin grows up, he becomes a divinely inspired poet and has a son whom he calls Oscar, a name that means "he who loves the deer." According to legend, Oisin eventually joins his mother, the Deer Goddess, Sadv, in the Other World.

According to scholars, this Deer Goddess, Sadv, is linked to another ancient goddess, Artemis, Mistress of Wild Animals. In Greek legend it was said that pregnant does swam to an island sacred to Artemis, Goddess of Birth-Giving, to bear their young. Originally, Artemis was the sun goddess of early times, along with her mother, Leto. Artemis represented the young, rising sun while her mother represented the old setting sun. Later, with the rise of the patriarchy, Artemis was relegated to the night realm as the moon goddess, while her male counterpart, Apollo, became the solar divinity. A sun god replaced the sun goddess. Artemis was also linked to the earlier Scythian goddess Diana, a sun goddess of the pre-Indo-European peoples and the ancient tribes of the steppes. It is probable that the Arctic peoples' practices and beliefs in a sun goddess and reindeer goddess spread southward to the people of the steppes and eventually through Europe to the Mediterranean sometime during the Ice Age.[7]

The Sami people considered the sun to be a mother to all

living creatures. The reindeer were children of the sun mother who preserved her reindeer offspring, which she offered as gifts to humankind, and brought natural warmth to them so they could fare well. The sun gave light, warmth, fertility, and beautiful weather for the reindeer's benefit. And when the Sami people were lost in the mountains, they prayed to the sun for her light and rays to see their way home. Since the Sami people saw the sun as a mother goddess, they sacrificed young reindeer does, preferably white ones, to her. They believed that the sacrificed reindeer would receive its body and life again and return to the earth as a bigger and more beautiful animal.[8]

There are many statues and pictures of Artemis standing alongside or touching her great antlered deer. Gallic-Roman iconography also depicts women with deer antlers. A statue in the British Museum of a seated goddess, most likely honoring Sadv, has a fully human face with antlers sprouting from her hair. The antlered deer accompanying Artemis, who was also a birth deity, are considered by many male historians to be stags, and the antlered hinds in fairy tales and art are viewed as an anomaly or interpreted as female with the attributes of a male. But many women would consider this view erroneous, for female reindeer have antlers, authenticating the natural symbolism of the antlered deer goddesses and linking them with the ancient creatrix, the Reindeer Goddess. Hence, the deer goddess cult of the northern Europeans and the veneration of the Mediterranean Artemis most likely descends directly from the ancient Reindeer Goddess of the Arctic.

According to the archaeologist Marija Gimbutas, the deer is one of the primary forms of the birth-giving goddess.[9] As creatrix of life, guardian of birth-giving, and protectress of the reindeer, the Reindeer Goddess has power so great that she brings the sun for the cycle of the seasons, so that in spring the ice melts and the reindeer can travel to give birth. She is a deity that can protect and transform us.

Tibetan Buddhism honors a wisdom goddess of long life named Tseringma, who is linked with the reindeer. As depicted in a nineteenth-century Tibetan *thangka* painting from eastern Tibet, she holds a staff and mirror, implements of awakened presence. The staff represents her male consort who embodies skillful means. Tseringma rides a white antlered deer across the snow-capped peaks of the Tibetan mountains and is surrounded by an entourage of women riders, "sister" wisdom beings, who are able to help all sentient beings in any circumstance.

Men are also graced by dreams that reveal the dignity of the Reindeer Goddess and that remind them of her healing energy. In Keith's dream of the Reindeer Woman, her healing presence was more powerful to him than a roomful of doctors. Scott, a sensitive man in his forties, also dreamed of the Reindeer Goddess. In the dream Scott was walking in the forest when he came to a clearing where he saw a hunter about to shoot a deer. Scott walked between the hunter and the deer and told the man to put down his gun. Surprised, the hunter did as Scott said, then left. When Scott turned around to look at the deer, a beautiful woman with antlers on her head stood where the deer had been. She came up to Scott to thank him, looked soulfully into his eyes, and kissed him deeply on the lips. When Scott awoke, he felt blessed and reaffirmed in his life.

Women who dream of deer with antlers, or paint themselves with antlers on their heads, invoke the powers and qualities of the Reindeer Goddess, thereby glimpsing their own divinity. A woman named Karina had the following dream:

> I am driving through the countryside in a convertible. To my left birds are carrying in their beaks a tapestry of leaves and lay it in a sunlit field that reflects golden light. Just ahead of me in the middle of the road looms a huge golden goddess. To my left, beside the car and running with it, are animals—a bear, a wolf, an elk, and a deer, which I know is feminine but which wears a large rack of antlers. The goddess speaks: "These animals are for you. They will not harm you."

The golden goddess, who is reminiscent of the sun goddess and the Lady of the Beasts, carried a message to Karina that was important not only to her personally but to us all: If we are open to nature, as Karina is in the dream, driving a convertible car open to the sky, able to see and appreciate the birds, the leaves, and the golden light, we too can see and hear the goddess who is willing to share the munificent animal energies with us.

As a daughter of the sun, the golden Sami sun goddess, Beijen-neite, who was created from a smile and a tear of joy, comes to the people of Lapland to help them in a similar way. When the people have forgotten how to care for the reindeer, Beijen-neite comes to earth in human form and teaches them how to care for her holy animals. Rather than punishing the people, in the manner of an angry patriarchal god, Beijen-neite teaches with kindness. She shows the people how to milk the holy *vajas* and how to tame the wild deer. She teaches the people how to make clothes from the reindeer's skin, how to utilize their tendons as thread, and how to craft necessary tools and objects from the animals she cherishes. She inspires the people and enlivens them with poems and songs that hail the treasured deer.

In the spirit of the Reindeer Goddess, contemporary women write poems in praise of the reindeer. Mary Elizabeth Williams wrote the following poem while she was on Kodiak Island, Alaska, where she was living and working with the native Yupik Eskimo women who make reindeer dancing fans. After Williams had written several poems honoring the reindeer, she learned that her great-grandmother was a full-blooded Laplander, a fact that had been suppressed by her family for several generations. In her poem "The Fan Maker," she thanks the reindeer spirits for their gifts.

THE FAN MAKER

I have beautiful dancing fans.
I made them myself.
They have a place of honor
On my household shelf.
The reindeer gave me a special gift—
Their long and silky hair.
It is the lace work in my fan,
Swaying gently in the air.
It graces a base of sea grass
That I picked and dried in the sun.
I wove and wound them carefully—
Honoring each one
With the benediction of my hands
That still know the old ways.
I'll be making dancing fans

The rest of my earthly days.
I give thanks for the gift of the reindeer
And the grasses of the sea
And to the spirit
That gave the fan making gift to me.[10]

Women artists who venerate the Reindeer Goddess energy in our time by painting portraits of themselves and other women with antlers branching from their heads include not only Frida Kahlo but Lee Lawson, Charleen Touchette, Susan Seddon Boulet, and Christine DeCamp.[11] These contemporary artists paint women standing by deer, riding the reindeer, or seated in a chariot drawn by deer, pictures reminiscent of ancient statues and paintings that are a tribute to the Deer Goddess. Artistic homage from antiquity includes a painting of deer and dancing priestesses from the Indus Valley civilization that are linked in a ritual with sun symbols and rosettes from Harappa, India, 2500–1500 B.C.E., and a Greek sculpture in which the goddess stands at the center of a cart guarded by deer with enormous antlers, found in Austria, from the seventh century B.C.E.[12]

Charleen Touchette, a French Canadian and North American Blackfoot Indian artist, has painted a series she calls *Reindeer Mother Visions.* In one painting, entitled "Deer Mother Vision," a beautiful bare-breasted, long-haired, antlered, human-faced mother gazes at her child with love while the beams of light between the mother's eye and that of her baby reveal the stream of energy interchanged between the personal and the mythic Reindeer Woman mother and the newborn infant. Touchette's other paintings depict mythic mothers—the Sky Mother and the reindeer-antlered Sun Mother—settling her newborn babe upon the earth. The image of the Reindeer Woman, which appeared to Charleen Touchette in a personal vision, expresses the magic of motherhood as well as her own artistic creations.

Like the ancient women artists in Neolithic times who sat together in a room below the temple creating artworks for the tabernacle, generations of matriarchal North American Indian women in Touchette's family sit together in a room today, creating artworks as a reservoir of spiritual sustenance. In *The Reflowering of the Goddess,* Gloria Orenstein points out that Touchette's work, painted in brilliant primary colors that emit energy fields of light, is reminiscent of the Huichol yarn paintings and rejoins us with the creative forces of the cosmos. She says that Touchette's Native American vision helps us remember that the Great Mothers—"mythic, spiritual, and real"—ultimately give rise to all life and empower it, imparting their blessings upon future generations. Orenstein adds that art itself can be understood metaphorically as a kind of Reindeer Mother. Art blesses us with energy and vision, reconnecting us to all those mythic and maternal realms that give unique meaning to our human world. The Reindeer Mother's energy engenders acts of love and vision in a weaving of female energy which, as life and art, together create the "Beauty Way."[13]

In dreams the reindeer may bless with her presence, allowing the dreamer to see her and approach. One woman dreamed that a female reindeer, accompanied by two smaller deer, came up and kissed her on the lips. The dreamer felt holy awe before the reindeer's mystical coming. Another woman dreamed that she was in the depths of a great forest. In a clearing was a wooden trough where the reindeer came to drink. She was chosen to fill the trough with water for the reindeer. After pouring water for the reindeer, she awoke with joyful tears, basking in a feeling of love and tenderness that enveloped her in radiant, glowing warmth.

Steven, a man in his fifties, was depressed over the break-up of a relationship and felt he had to choose a new direction for his life. He dreamed he was in the midst of a blue fog, but heard a voice that told him to walk through it and he'd be fine. Passing through the fog, he saw a beautiful golden city glittering on his right. Although he was drawn toward it, he felt he should go through a barn on his left instead. Now he was dressed like the fool in the Tarot and realized he was being followed by a small herd of deer. Seeing them reflected in a pulsating membrane before him, he realized they were reindeer. As he and the reindeer looked deep into each others eyes, he felt warm and loved. The wonderful feeling of love that passed between Steven and the reindeer assured him that he would emerge from his depression and that his life was heading in the right direction.

Connie, a therapist, confided that she had been feeling so emotionally exhausted and burnt out that she was worried that she would be unable to continue in her profession. But then she had a dream that relieved her anxiety, comforted her, and gave her hope that she could sustain her restorative work. In the dream a voice said: "You have the gifts of the reindeer and the buffalo." The dream reminded her of the healing powers of Buffalo Woman, who brought the gift of the peace pipe, and of the Reindeer Goddess, who nurtures life. Both spirits commemorate the regenerative gift we all have to offer—to respect ourselves, others, and all existence through a peaceful and compassionate way of being.

When modern women and men are presented with the knowledge of the ancient Reindeer Goddess as a maternal divinity, presiding over life and death, they can invoke her spirit to help them on their spiritual journeys. As birth-giving journeyers, reindeer are especially endowed to help us along the path. Remembering inspiring experiences with deer in nature brings many people a feeling of serenity. For some, seeing deer brings comfort at a time of suffering and offers them a moment of healing. Others feel joy when they encounter deer's beauty and grace.

Meeting deer brings many people a moment of awe, in which they feel the presence of the goddess. Whenever I encounter a deer on my walks through the wilds, I feel blessed, the recipient of Nature's largess. I pause, become fully present, and pray in thanks, wondering what hidden meaning will be revealed as I gaze into its eyes. To me, the deer is a sacred guide that beckons me to care for my soul and reminds me of the ancient mysteries entrusted to us by the animals. When I see one, I feel free, as though the deer goddess had caressed my spirit, reminding me of the gifts of creation and my dignity as a woman. After a deer leaps away, I follow it in my imagination, grateful for its generous bestowal.

The Even people's reindeer goddess, whose being connotes a way without stress, offers an image for healing in our time, since stress is one of the major factors contributing to so many diseases, physical and mental. The Reindeer Goddess's way is not without struggle, since the life of the reindeer is difficult. But struggle differs from stress—the strain that is unresolved and turns back on the body. When stress gets in the way, it actually takes our attention away from spiritual life and causes us to lose ourselves in worry. To live a spiritual life requires that we endure the tension of spirit and matter, the eternal and the finite, life and death. When we are overburdened by stress, we tend to cling compulsively to one of these poles. We try to act as though life and death were not inextricable wedding partners, members of a more encompassing whole.

Khinken, the Even's reindeer goddess who presides over the life and death of animals and humans, is an image that we can invoke for reducing stress, healing the heart, and living in harmony with nature. The goddess reflects the Even's way of life as they follow nature's cycles, accepting life and death as a whole. In contrast to the dualistic thinking that dominates the industrial world, splitting organic reality into irreconcilable opposites such as the good and the bad, the beautiful and the ugly, and life and death and separating human life from that of the animals, the Even's goddess honors all being as part of the great mystery of wholeness.

Healing images of female antlered deer have appeared to modern women and men who are stricken with cancer and other illnesses. Suzanne Lovell, an art and movement therapist, has recorded in a video how a spontaneous image of a Reindeer Woman came to her and became an integral healing image in her own recovery from cancer. At a conference on shamanism and healing for women, she related that after being diagnosed with cancer she danced spontaneously around a pole in the center of a room in which sat other women witnessing her. As she danced around the pole, a symbol for the world pole that unites the upper, earthly, and lower realms, she felt her arms branching into antlers. Later she painted a number of dreams and visions in which a deer woman with antlers sprouting from her head came to her as a goddess of healing.[14]

She is one of a number of women who have shared accounts of healing in which the image of a reindeer woman appears. For example, a doctor from Denmark told me that one of his patients began to recover after seeing a reindeer vision that gave her hope. A man in recovery from prostate cancer told me that a deer came to him in a vision and became a source for his healing. An American woman, in early recovery from addiction, told of seeing a stag and doe in front of her parents' house in the Blue Ridge Mountains. Later, as she took a walk through the fields at dusk, she noticed a flash of something light on the ground. Bending over, she discovered a newly shed three-point antler which she felt was the antler of the deer that she had seen two days earlier. She said: "This experience was deeply affecting and moves me still. I bleached the antler, and it now sits on the altar in my bedroom with the candles, incense, and Buddha. I meditate upon the antler as a form of 'spiritual wiring' that connects me with universal energies. The end that points to me connects me to the points that reach to the heavens. The antlers are a beautiful reminder of the healing energies that saved my life and brought me back into the world."

Honoring the presence of the mystical Reindeer Goddess invites us to imagine the Reindeer Woman, who can serve as a contemporary healing image for modern women and men. If we follow her, she can lead us into the forest, a place of mystery, away from linear roads that lead to worn out places or to dead-ends of ecological destruction. It is in the forest that we may connect with our own individual way, the life we are meant to follow. The Reindeer Woman can be a muse for our creative imagination, a muse in whom nature and spirit are wed. Aware that humans are one of nature's miracles, she can lead us to new spaces where we can surrender the urge to control and possess so that the thrill of the unexpected can happen.

The Reindeer Woman is nomadic. She presents us with the wandering life, a process guided by the rhythms of the body. Feeling the heartbeat, the breath, the graceful stride, the leap, she leads us to connect with our original urge to create. We come into our own time—not the clock's tick-tock of technological time, which compresses space, uses us, and constricts our every movement. Rather, following her, we wander into the wondering time of meditative awareness, silence, solitude, and seclusion. It is quiet there, so we can hear the wind sing through the leaves of the birch, heed the rustle of grasses, and listen to our own birdsong. We can feel the sun warm our skin, smell the evergreens' aroma, touch the furry moss, and stroke the bird's feather. We can see the tenuous thread that the spider has woven into a web of creation that astounds us with its strangeness and wonder.

Running in a trance with the pregnant reindeer, we learn endurance, how to pace ourselves for pregnancy—giving birth to earthly and spiritual existence. Following these antlered messengers, we see through the visible world into the invisible sphere. In the center of the Arctic rose, the Reindeer Woman sees the threshold to the soul. Her antlers receive lavish, lightning visions, transmuting them into messages of healing and wisdom for the people. Wild and wondrous, her spirituality resides in nature, not apart from it. She knows the need for grounding; she honors the spirits of a place. Her heart drums the music of the earth. She is the heartbeat within the ground of all living things. She throbs with grief when the world is torn asunder; her heart vibrates with joy when she sees us loving the earth. Her tears melt the ice of frozen feelings when we are cut off from our mother, the earth. A guide to the gentle, she transmits clairvoyance, leading us to quest for harmony and peace. Her antlers conduct the rhythm of her heart, and songs spring through them to the stars. She leaps through the crossing of the worlds, giving birth to the journeying nature of our souls.

Eight

THE WOUNDED
DEER

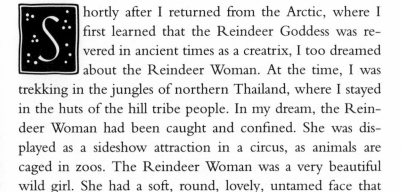hortly after I returned from the Arctic, where I first learned that the Reindeer Goddess was revered in ancient times as a creatrix, I too dreamed about the Reindeer Woman. At the time, I was trekking in the jungles of northern Thailand, where I stayed in the huts of the hill tribe people. In my dream, the Reindeer Woman had been caught and confined. She was displayed as a sideshow attraction in a circus, as animals are caged in zoos. The Reindeer Woman was a very beautiful wild girl. She had a soft, round, lovely, untamed face that seemed to express the same natural spontaneity of the peaceful Sami people. Her long black hair was piled on top of her head in the fashion of some of the Thai hill tribe women,

who are frequently taken from their people and abused as prostitutes in Bangkok, or dressed up as tourist attractions in areas around Chiangmai. In the dream, I knew it was my task to make others conscious of the Reindeer Woman's mistreatment and try to free her.

My dream of the Reindeer Woman, who was caged and humiliated as a sideshow oddity, fit into a striking pattern that I was discovering as I researched the reindeer. In stories and dreams I gathered about the reindeer spirit, during workshops on the theme of feminine spirituality, woman after woman from around the world spoke not only of dreams but of incidents from waking life that related to the image of the wounded deer. Both the dreams and the actual events revealed abuse to a gentle and peaceful feminine way of being that these women experienced as essential to themselves.

Like these women, I had experienced attacks from bullies at times when I was vulnerable and openhearted. What is it, I began to wonder, that leads bullies to want to wound vulnerable people or gentle creatures like the deer? What kind of impulse wants to destroy their beauty and spirit? Whenever and wherever beauty exists, is there also a dark force waiting to hurt and maim or even obliterate it? Is this dark shadow why we are so afraid to be vulnerable? For as a culture, we certainly are adverse to showing true feelings and sensitivity. We tend to adapt an armored toughness that masks our flaws, disguises our humanness, and makes us appear impregnable.

Our cultural aversion to *vulnerability* is evidenced by the synonyms one finds in the thesaurus for this word—*handicap, burden, liability, misfortune, encumbrance, disadvantage, exposed, unsafe, precarious, insecure, unprotected*—all words with a negative connotation. Our society's cultural dualism splits apart qualities of strength and vulnerability, categorizing people, races, and nations either by power or by weakness. We are a wounded society, attacker and victim alike. Thus, the wounded deer is an image for us all.

Perhaps vulnerability attracts attackers yet frightens them because their own pregnable, open side has been abused. We now know that the abused child often grows into an abusive adult. People who are bullies may themselves have been taken advantage of, their own creative forces used by others, or discounted and ignored. To protect themselves, they have learned to attack first, assaulting ones they sense are weaker than themselves.

When people are cruel to others, most often they're intolerant of their own vulnerability. People who are afraid to feel the pain and suffering of their own hurt often abuse those who reveal similar injuries, as if wounding others could shield them from themselves. When they begin to face their pain, they may abuse whomever is nearest. They make the mistake of equating strength with toughness and vulnerability with victimhood, instead of seeing the potency of openness.

Attitudes like acquisitiveness and literal thinking, which try to hold on to concrete objects, ideas, and power, would naturally fear the ephemeral deer that can move so swiftly between the visible and invisible worlds. Holding such attitudes prevents us from seeing that the state of being pregnable is actually a strength—if we are conscious of how to be in this condition. It means being open to giving birth, the very instinctual purpose that drives the reindeer and all of us on our respective paths. The person who attacks another's vulnerability is also violating his own receptivity, violating her own birth-giving self.

One can see this happening in the creative process. The

critic who attacks another's creative work or life unfairly, or judges it in an untimely way, is often the person who is afraid to dare to attempt to create in his or her own life. Fearful of exposing or actualizing their own potentialities, their inner critic assaults their own creative impulses as harshly as they berate the efforts of others. And if they do take the risk to embody their creative vision, they sometimes destroy their own work by tearing up the poem or the painting, or by neglecting it by hiding it in a closet or desk drawer. The very qualities that we assault in others, we also assail in ourselves and our shared humanity.

Similarly, the unthinking, instinctual push to flee from threatening situations, to run away from attackers rather than to hold one's ground and stand up for one's rights and integrity, reveals the darker side of the deer image that reflects a commensurate fear of openness. Paradoxically, another dark side of the deer is revealed when a person appears innocent, without a balanced conscious awareness of the shadow side of life. When a reindeer mother uses her antlers to stand her ground and protect herself and her young from predators, she reveals a balance between vulnerability and strength, between gentleness and self-protection.

In nature, animal predators such as the wolf are not evil beings. Animal predators rarely kill more prey than they need for food. Wolves live in families and can be gentle and nurturing to one another. In the Arctic, which they inhabit along with the reindeer, they tend to take the easiest catch for their prey. According to local lore, if a wolf is tracking a reindeer and the deer looks straight into the wolf's eye, the wolf will not attack it.

The following dream reveals both attraction to the deer's vulnerability and fear of it. The dream image came to Kimberly, a musician and songwriter, who identifies with the free and gentle spirit of the deer and who loves the primitive freedom of running long distances in the wilderness, where she feels serenity, rejuvenation, and the freedom to be her feminine self.

> I am in a thickly forested wilderness. As I gaze through the trees and undergrowth, the head of a young deer emerges from within the camouflage of the woods. There is something very powerful and magical about the way the deer's head and neck have emerged so silently from the forest. I can see the deer's moist black nose and the quivering of its nostrils and ears as it performs its survival ritual of hypervigilant scanning for any signs of threat or danger. The deer's image conveys a sense of purity, gentleness, and vulnerability. At the same time, it conveys power and the energy to bolt and run; to merge and disappear into the safety of the wilderness. I gaze at the deer for what seems like an instant as well as an eternity. The deer's eyes meet mine, and I feel as if I am looking into my own soul. I experience a vulnerability that frightens me. The instant I experience this fear, the young deer bolts and runs and disappears into the safety and camouflage of the forest. As the young deer disappears, I feel a sense of something that I long to embrace but cannot grasp, except for an instant, because of the fear that the deer's vulnerability evokes in me.

In Kimberly's dream, meeting the deer's eyes means looking into her own soul. In a moment of truth, the gaze of the deer challenges us. Whenever we open our heart and soul in truth, we *are* vulnerable. To create, to relate, to be human calls us to be genuine and visible. And this exposes us to the possibility of the wound.

Women who open themselves up to others, only to be assaulted in one form or another, often feel like wounded deer. Wounds to our psyches, as well as to the deer, come in different forms. They may be experienced when we are not heard by others, when we are judged unfairly, when we are manipulated, when we are maligned, or when we do not defend ourselves. Often we mistreat the sensitive part of ourselves, the sites of old wounds, then judge ourselves as failures. More obvious, and all too prevalent, are cases in which, just by being who we are, we are physically harassed, abused, or raped. We do not invite this abuse, but sometimes, because of our human attributes and the potential to be vulnerable, we are targeted by dark forces to suffer. Yet if we are to learn and to grow, we must accept our suffering. It is part of being human and living fully.

Some women who identify with the wounded deer tell stories of actual traumatic experiences with hunter fathers who taunted their daughters by flaunting a bloody deer that they had killed. Perhaps the most horrifying deer-hunting memory is related by Charleen. When she was only six years old, her father taught her to hunt small animals. When she was ten, her father took her deer hunting and forced her to take up a gun against her will and try to shoot a deer. Although the rifle was bigger than she was, Charleen managed to shoot and kill a six-point buck. Proud of his daughter, her father brought the dead deer home and made her help him gut and skin it. This nauseated Charleen, and she vomited. In a drunken rage her father said, "If that makes you sick, see how you like this," and forced her to perform oral sex on him. These events occurred in a small cabin behind their house, a place where Charleen had often played with her toys. Later, her mother prepared the dead elk for dinner and her father forced her to eat the meat. The antlered deer head was hung high on the dining-room wall as a trophy of Charleen's hunting victory.

Charleen said that this was the first of repeated sexual violations by her father. She has been dealing with its injurious consequences ever since. As an adolescent, she had to live with the deer head hanging on the wall in her house, a constant reminder of the trauma. At fourteen, she started to drink, and suffered alcoholism until she went into recovery at thirty-four. Through the process of recovery, Charleen was able to work through these early wounds and eventually entered a healing profession to help other wounded women. She has been in recovery for twenty-one years.

The wounded deer is symbolic of abuses of the human spirit. Often it is directly related to sexual abuse. Antlers are associated with sexuality because male deer use them in sexual communication to attract the does and to frighten off their rivals. Male antlers have a special scent that attracts female deer. In their velvet stage, antlers are desired by humans for their aphrodisiac qualities, and some people acquire them illegally by killing deer in early summer, then making the velvet antlers into erotic potions sold for financial gain.

Some men are so intrigued by antlers that they kill deer simply to hang these crowns in their homes as trophies; such hunters are captive to their own greed. They prize antlers much in the way certain men seek beautiful women as signs of their success, power, or sexual prowess. The very antlers that inspire some people with awe at nature's wonder provoke in others the desire for ownership and the lust for control.[1]

Just as the allure of antlers as erotic stimulant, coveted

trophy, ornament, or sign of sexual power can lead people to poach deer, the same antlers and their fascination can arouse disrespect and boorishness that dishonor female integrity. The deer-hunting culture, when not based on respect for nature, leads to a debasing of women and other misogynist behavior. At its worst, this attitude may result in sexual molestation, as it did for Charleen.

Women who live in areas where deer-hunting season is a time for drunken celebrations have told me of their fear and aversion to the crude behavior that can accompany this sport. At night, in one of these areas, a bar called Buckeye advertises with a neon sign that displays an image of a martini glass containing a glowing red cherry and flashing red antlers that extend from the sides of the martini glass. To many, the cherry alludes both to the deer's eye and to women's sexuality, and the extending antlers suggest the blood-red velvet antler that is used for aphrodisiacs and the phallic potency of antlers and hunters. To some, conquering a deer represents conquering a woman.

Disrespectful, illegal deer hunting is offensive to responsible hunters who love deer, who abide by hunting ethics, and who feel a spiritual affinity with the antlered animals, as the reindeer people do. Poaching and violating the hunting ethic worry hikers and nature lovers of both sexes who must avoid walks in the woods during hunting season for fear of being shot or injured. Just yesterday, while I was hiking up a well-used jeep road with a good friend, we saw two used cartridge shells on the trail. I had checked with the ranger station beforehand and was told that on this particular day hunting was illegal since it was a transitional time in the hunting season. The ranger added that it was illegal to shoot across trails and roads at deer. However, the ranger warned me about "buck fever"—the addiction to killing a deer, which is as lethal as any mania that possesses the soul and deprives a person of judgment. Under the influence of buck fever, hunters often become their own victims, wounding or killing each other through blunders. A friend of mine told me that his father, who hunted to provide food for the family, had been shot by another hunter a number of years ago and was wounded so severely that he was unable to work again. Recently, the local news reported that on a foggy day a hunter thought he saw a deer and fired. When he went to collect the quarry, he found that he had killed his son by mistake.

Consider the story of Simone, a French woman who loved to be in nature. One day while she was a foreign student in an American college, Simone was walking through the woods, enjoying the brilliant beauty of the changing autumn leaves. At one point, she came upon a hunter with a gun. Thinking she was safe, she continued to cherish the golden fire of the leaves—the last thing she remembered before awakening to find herself in a hospital severely injured. She had been attacked and her skull bashed by the butt of the unknown hunter's gun. After learning about how she had been hurt, Simone had a healing dream that she had been taken into the nurturing body of Mother Earth, a motif that appears in the healing dreams of many men and women. Gathered deep into the earth's body of fallen leaves and mud, Simone was reborn in the dream.

Although the dream helped heal the trauma to her psyche, ever since then Simone has been very conscious of the paradox of good and evil, and the dilemma of innocence and injustice in the world. The deer had always been an animal with which she felt a soul kinship, since she related to its innocence and gentleness. Now she was alerted to be aware of the threat to innocence and to the attraction that instigates some people to want to affront naïveté and to attack those who are open, as though they were moving targets.

Just as Charleen and Simone suffered brutal treatment from deer hunters and seem themselves like wounded deer, so the wounded deer in women's dreams is an image that reveals injuries to our vulnerable and compassionate hearts and our feminine spirit. For example, Maureen, a woman in her forties, told the following dream:

> I am in a kitchen with three men and am very angry with them because they are not feeding the animals—a female grizzly bear and a female reindeer with small antlers. I am horrified to see that the reindeer has been severely wounded. Her head has been cut off, but luckily she is still alive.

This dream initiated a turning point for Maureen, who had been neglecting her feelings, especially her emotions regarding sexual relationships with men. Maureen said she tended to jump into bed on the first date with men to whom she was attracted, thus cutting off the chance to allow these relationships to develop more gradually and mature. At these times, she forgot to listen to the subtle wisdom of her instincts and her heart.

The dream alerted Maureen to her anger about her behavior, even though her anger was directed toward the men who failed to notice and to value her vulnerability. She was able to acknowledge her anger at her own failure to feed and nurture the female grizzly bear and for having been unable to protect the injured reindeer. Maureen identified with the female bear as a totem animal that represented her power while the reindeer symbolized her tender feelings, a side of herself that she tended to neglect. Although the reindeer was seriously wounded, the dream gave Maureen the consolation that at least it was alive and therefore could be healed. The severing of the reindeer's head suggested that she needed to reattach her head to her body and use her instinctive intelligence to protect her feelings. The dream constituted a turning point in Maureen's life, she said, alerting her to the need to value her gentle spirit and to beware of violating her soul through indiscriminate sex.

Dreams of wounded deer that I have heard include images of deer that are tied up, bound by ropes and chains, caught in traps, tangled in thickets, or confined in pens or fences. Some wounded-deer dreams show deer being attacked by predators, hit by automobiles, mutilated, or shot by guns or arrows. One woman reported a dream in which she saw a herd of reindeer flying freely across the sky, but someone from the ground was shooting at them. Another woman shared a dream in which she was driving along a highway; her car was stopped, and she was forced to gaze at the corpse of a deer that had been viciously killed.

These last two dreams alerted both women to the necessity of understanding the meaning of such horrible sights on the personal, cultural, and universal levels. The threat to the gentle deer, they felt, symbolized the peril to personal feelings, the jeopardy to women's tenderness and vulnerability, and the hazard for our human capacity for kindness and compassion.

While our deer wounds may come originally from our external circumstances, such as parental upbringing or society's devaluation of the feminine, our hope for healing these wounds lies ultimately within ourselves. We need to value the strengths of the deer—its graceful sensitivity and openness of heart. Yet we also need to be alert to the ways in which we may collude with its attackers, who count on our tendency to be naive or to flee without defense. Once the transformation has begun, we can share with one another the ways we have found to heal ourselves.

A striking image of the wounded deer appeared in a dream of Sherry, a woman who was addicted to romance. On Valentine's Day, Sherry dreamed that she opened a fortune cookie and saw a picture of a large reindeerlike animal, drawn in black on a white place mat. The hind section of the deer was gone, devoured by the jaws of a giant black scorpionlike creature. The dream came during a negative point in a romantic relationship. Sherry felt that the devouring jaws were an image of the voracious romance addiction that unconsciously gripped her and that was eating away at her deer instincts—her innate capacity to find a relationship guided by her heart. At that time, she was feeling tense, fearful, and devoured by inertia, an aspect of the romance addiction.

Upon awakening from the dream, Sherry remembered a fairy tale, "The Girl and the Evil Spirit," which she had been reading.[2] In this Siberian story, a reindeer herdswoman wanders alone on the tundra, singing magic songs to keep her reindeer with her, when suddenly a gigantic pair of jaws reaches out from an open abyss extending from heaven to earth. She hurls a staff onto the ground to delay the jaws; then she runs for safety, throwing a comb and a red handkerchief over her shoulder. The comb turns into a forest and the red handkerchief into a fire; they delay the pursuing jaws. But then the jaws devour the forest and spout water onto the fire. The herdswoman changes into four animals, each one faster than the one before, and finally she reaches a white tent and collapses onto the earth. When she awakens, she finds that the evil spirit pursuing her has changed into a handsome and kindly man, who offers her the choice of himself and his three younger brothers to wed. The herdswoman chooses the transformed man standing before her.

The heroic reindeer herdswoman uses the special qualities she has learned from living on the tundra with the reindeer to defend herself against the threatening jaws, and she changes her life from one that lacked human companionship to one that includes a healthy human relationship. For Sherry, she served as a model. The devouring jaws, symbolic of demonic forces in the unconscious, suggest an insatiable obsession, like the romance addiction from which Sherry, the dreamer, suffered and which cut her off from a relationship.

In the magic songs that bond the fairy-tale heroine with the reindeer, she expresses the images that rise up from her unconscious, images that can help a heroine on her journey toward transformation. The songs also indicate the richness of her cultural ancestry as a source of meaning and creativity.

In the fairy tale, the reindeer woman confronts the threatening situation. The staff that she hurls onto the ground symbolizes power and conscious discretion. She is active on her own behalf, conscious but also instinctive because she has the sense of direction she needs to escape the omnivorous forces. The herdswoman runs from the jaws and throws objects over her shoulder in order to gain speed and mobility. As she sacrifices possessions and nonessential attachments, they change into obstacles for her pursuer.

The herdswoman's nomadic life with the reindeer on the tundra has given her the strength of simplicity and the instincts for survival on a difficult journey. Her love for the reindeer has given her a direct relationship with nature. She knows the ways of Mother Earth. Thus, the comb that she throws behind her turns into a forest. Sacrificing the comb means surrendering the desire for perfect order, since the comb straightens the hair on our heads. It can also mean surrendering overattention to oneself, to one's outer image, one's vanity or self-absorption, out of which we, like the herdswoman, have to grow. Relinquishing the red handkerchief, in turn, signifies letting go of the consuming emotions with which one can become obsessed, like feeling so rejected in a relationship that the rest of one's life is paralyzed by jealousy or revenge. The herdswoman's ability to surrender possessions allows her to be free to run like the reindeer.

Trusting her animal energies, a reliance necessary for survival on the Arctic tundra, the heroine surrenders herself to her instincts for survival. She is then able to outrun the threatening jaws, just as the reindeer can outrun its predators. Through her heroic journey, made possible by yielding to the ways of nature, she transforms the demon that pursues her into a chivalrous man. In the same way, people who are pursued by the demons of addiction can recover if they are able to surrender their obsession in order to see the human qualities in themselves and the people around them. Recovery is transformation, a never-ending process, just as the reindeer journey begins again just when it seems to be over.

The dream of the wounded reindeer alerted Sherry to the dangers of her devouring romance addiction. The fairy tale contains an image of redemption—the reindeer herdswoman, a heroine who is able to escape the evil spirit pursuing her and, as a result of her conscious and natural actions, consummate a divine wedding with a loving man. That the fairy-tale heroine chose to try to elude the evil spirit emphasized to Sherry that she herself had a choice. Either she could remain a victim and be devoured by a dysfunctional relationship, or she could choose transformation. The fairy-tale heroine's transcendent link with her reindeer, her magic songs, and Nature's ways symbolized for Sherry the sacred relationship to the divinity within herself for which she yearned.

Facing the demons in ourselves is a task for all of us, in whatever culture we may live. These demons can come in the form of addictions, as in the case of Sherry, or in the form of emotional attitudes such as envy, cynicism, and resentments, which close our hearts and restrict our vision or pit us against one another. To help in such moments, the Lakota people believe that the Great Mystery expresses itself through the spirit guide.

To the Chukchi people, who live at the top of the world in Siberia above the Arctic Circle and who believe they are descendants of the reindeer, the reindeer spirit guide helps people face the demonic powers of the Moon Man. There, where high winds sweep from the North Pole across the bare tundra and the frightening face of the ghostly moon stares severely through the ocean fog and winter night's frost, they tell the following folk tale, "The Girl and the Moon Man."[3] In this story, the reindeer is a helpful animal that protects its mistress, a reindeer herdress, against the fearsome Moon Man, who kidnaps animals and young maidens and symbolizes the abusive predators that want to wound the deer.

One night, when the Moon Man sets his sights upon a reindeer herdress, her reindeer warns her to beware of the moon. The reindeer protects the young woman by hiding her in a snowbank, which it digs up with its hoof, turning the snow into a hill. When the Moon Man comes to carry off the girl, he can't find her. The reindeer carries her back to her home, running as fast as it can. Then it asks her to sit on the fire, and it turns the girl into a lamp.

When the Moon Man enters the girl's house, he looks everywhere for her, but he doesn't approach the lamp, because he knows that if the two fires meet, they will burn each other up. After the Moon Man leaves the house, the girl calls to him, and he looks for her once more, but again he cannot find her. Weary now, the Moon Man starts to shrivel. The girl grabs him and ties him up. Afraid she will kill him, the Moon Man begs her to release him. In return, he promises to light up the sky for the people and to mark off the months in order to measure the year.

To protect herself in case the Moon Man wants to come after her once he is free, the girl refuses to release him immediately and questions him carefully. But the Moon Man now knows he is no match for the reindeer herdress and tells her that she has too much spirit for him to capture. He promises that he will never leave his upper path again. With this assurance the girl lets the Moon Man go to light up the sky. Thanks to the reindeer herdress and her guide, the reindeer, the people now know when it is the time of the Moon of the Old Bucks, the Moon of the Cold Udders, the Full Udder Moon, the Moon of the Calves, the Moon of the Waters, the Moon of the New Leaves, the Warm Moon, the Moon of the Rubbing of Antlers, the Moon of the Light Frost, the Autumn Moon, the Moon of the Back, and the Moon of the Shrinking Days of Winter.

By confronting the Moon Man, the herdress, aided by her reindeer, enables the Chukchi people to measure the seasons by the months of the year, naming them according to the reindeer's link with the moon cycles. Through its magical powers, the reindeer protects her and guides her to find her inner strength and power to confront this demonic force. Just as the reindeer protects the herdress against the Moon Man's designs, so, for contemporary women, the reindeer image can serve as a guide to spiritual freedom, to help the soul preserve itself against demonic forces that want to wound the gentle feminine spirit and its doe wisdom.

In art, too, the image of the wounded deer reminds us powerfully of the potentiality for injury to the open heart. Expressing a wound through painting is a powerful way to try to heal it. Frida Kahlo's self-portrait as a wounded deer expressed her sense of betrayal by her husband, the painter Diego Rivera, whose womanizing and infidelity tortured her. Frida Kahlo suffered physically, too, from a horrendous bus accident that necessitated numerous surgeries. She painted *The Little Deer* just before undergoing a spinal fusion, and she presented the painting in thanks to two of her dearest friends, a couple who offered her affection and a home when she most needed it, and who, she felt, truly loved her for herself. She also gave them a ballad that she had written about the wounded deer that symbolized herself. Frida Kahlo had a pet fawn and felt the deer was her totemic animal since it embodied both the suffering of the Mater Dolorosa and the hope that heals. The Aztec, who believed in cosmic wholeness, called the deer tines "Kochitl," a name which means flowers and which she took for herself. In the ballad she wrote ". . . in the forest of the deer the sky is brightening."[4]

In the painting, Frida Kahlo is in a forest clearing that

reaches to the sea. The antlers on her human head have nine points, corresponding to the nine arrows that pierce her body—the body of a deer. The bloody wounds from the arrows suggest the bleeding heart, pierced by Cupid's arrow, the pain of love. At her feet lies a leafy broken branch from a young tree, which contrasts with the bare, gnarled, ancient tree trunks in rows that form the boundary of the clearing. In the background, the stormy sky is illuminated by lightning that reaches down into the sea.

The lightning looks like the antlers on her head and the branches of the tree—all suggesting the painter's revelatory relationship to the unconscious and to the spiritual world. The lightning, the antlers, the tree branches, and the arrows also point to the suffering that brings clarity, wisdom, transformation, and rebirth. The trees suggest the tree of life uniting the realms of heaven, earth, and the underworld or unconscious. The tree branch may also signify a pre-Columbian custom of putting a dry branch on a grave in order to help the deceased enter paradise, where the dry branch can be transformed into green leafy ones and the dead can be reborn. By painting *The Little Deer,* Frida Kahlo was able to express both the wound and a spiritual hope for healing.

Not only art but fairy tales reveal ways to heal the wounded self. In fairy tales, when a hunter saves a deer instead of killing it, the deer often thanks the hunter by offering to help him at a later time, when he needs aid. In the Siberian tale "Mergen and His Friends,"[5] Mergen, a daring Nanai hunter noted for his skill and for the fact that he never kills more animals than he needs, hunts long one day but finds no prey. Still hoping to find food for the night, he goes deep into the untamed taiga, where he comes upon a deer stranded in a swamp. Relieved that he has finally found a source of food, he is about to shoot an arrow at the animal, when suddenly the deer speaks to Mergen in a human voice. The deer asks him to spare it and to pull it out of the swamp. Listening to the deer's plea, Mergen is moved to save it. In gratitude, the deer tells him to call its name if he ever needs it, and it will come at once to his aid. Then the deer disappears in the forest, and Mergen continues on his way. Later, he also helps an ant and a sturgeon.

Mergen comes into a clearing, where he finds some tents and an old man from a strange clan. The old man invites Mergen into his tent, where the hunter sees a beautiful but sad maiden whose long black braid falls to her feet. Her melancholy smile pierces deep into his heart. Mergen feels a mysterious quality emanate from the lovely girl. In love with her, Mergen asks the old man to allow the maiden to be his wife. The old man warns Mergen that hundreds of bold hunters before him have sought her hand but failed. The men are now his servants. Still, he offers to set Mergen three tasks. If Mergen passes the tests, then he can become his son and marry the beautiful maiden, but if he fails, he will become a slave like the others. Immediately Mergen agrees to the challenge.

The old man orders his servants to bring his iron boots and tells Mergen that if he can wear out the boots in a single night, then he can return for the second task. The iron boots are so thick and heavy that Mergen thinks he would have to have a hundred lives and walk a hundred miles in each life to wear out the boots. But once he is back in the taiga, he remembers the deer's offer to come to his aid. When Mergen calls to his friend to help him, it appears before him at once. As soon as the deer hears of Mergen's plight, it puts the boots on its hind legs and runs off into the mountains so swiftly that it leaves a track of stars along the night sky. While the deer is running with the boots, Mergen lies down on the ground and falls asleep, and when he awakens at daybreak, the deer is by his side. The iron boots are so completely worn out that only the torn tops remain. Delighted, Mergen kisses the deer and hurries back with the boot-tops to the old man's tent. Flabbergasted, the old man assigns Mergen two more tasks. The second is to gather in one day every grain from five sacks of millet that have been thrown into the wind. The ant, with the help of the other ants of his tribe, helps Mergen complete this task. The third task is to find a golden ring that the old man's father has accidentally dropped into a river. The sturgeon that was befriended by Mergen retrieves the ring.

In amazement, the old man looks at the hunter, then goes into his tent and returns with his only daughter, offering the lovely maiden to Mergen to be his wife. He also tells Mergen to take his servants, his camp, and himself into his possession. To the old man's surprise, Mergen thanks him but replies that from this day on there will be no more servants. Instead, all will live as equals and in peace. This is Mergen's gift to the people. From that time, all the Nanai tribes along the shores of the Amur River have lived in peace and fellowship.

By helping the deer and the other animals, Mergen incorporates their qualities, especially the deer's compassionate heart, which enables him to abolish servitude and establish peace among the peoples. Mergen became conscious of this compassion through the task of wearing down the old man's heavy iron boots, symbolic of the iron domination that tyrannizes and enslaves others. Only the light-footed deer could run long enough and fast enough to shred the boots of the hard old man who captured his daughter's suitors and made them into servants. When the old man sees that Mergen has passed the test, he can think only in terms of ownership, so he offers himself and his servants to be Mergen's possessions. But Mergen, as a hunter who follows nature's way, is aware that too many possessions enslave people and prevent them from moving with ease. Instead of servitude, Mergen gives everyone freedom, peace, and harmony.

The story of Mergen shows the difference between the respectful hunter, who has a natural regard for animals and an ethics typical of indigenous hunters like the Reindeer People, and the greedy hunter, who may appear to be brave but really lusts for power or status. The figure of Mergen, a respectful hunter, contrasts with that of a power-hungry hunter like Agamemnon, king of Greece, who sacrifices his daughter Iphigenia through his pride.[6]

In Greek legend, the patriarch Agamemnon has pledged to wage war upon the barbarians of Troy because his brother's wife, the beautiful Helen, has been abducted by the Trojan, Paris. While the warships are assembling, Agamemnon disregards the boundaries of Artemis's hallowed forest by entering it and wounding one of her holy deer. In doing so he violates the free feminine spirit that the deer represents, dishonors the goddess, and provokes her wrath. Some legends report that Agamemnon adds to Artemis's ire by claiming that he is a greater hunter than the virgin goddess herself. Dishonored in this way by Agamemnon, the great goddess of the hunt has stilled the winds so that the warships heading for Troy cannot put to sea.

When the army is ready to sail for battle, there is no wind. The soldiers, crazed with lust to conquer, grow impatient and threaten Agamemnon's rule. Fearful that he will lose face before the angry men and forfeit all control, Agamemnon consults an oracle and is told to sacrifice his firstborn daughter, Iphigenia, to Artemis, if he wants the wind to blow. Then Greece can wage war.

Afraid that the angry men will revolt and usurp him, Agamemnon, in despair, decrees the sacrifice of the innocent Iphigenia. His gentle daughter pleads with him for her life, and her enraged mother, his wife, Clytemnestra, calls him a murderer, but the king refuses to change his judgment. Thus, for the sake of power, King Agamemnon kills the sacred deer and sacrifices his daughter. After conquering Troy, Agamemnon rapes Cassandra, the Trojan princess and prophetess (another wounded, deerlike woman) and takes her back to Greece as his slave. As Cassandra approaches the steps of Agamemnon's family house, she shrieks, "I smell blood," and faints. Clytemnestra, maddened by her husband's needless sacrifice of Iphigenia, clubs Cassandra to death and murders Agamemnon.

Agamemnon's story shows how the hunger for glory and power can lead to war, a heavy-handed addiction that takes control of consciousness and wounds or kills the gentle feminine. Agamemnon's need for dominance, and his inability to change his mind, is comparable to that of the old Siberian man who wore iron boots and enslaved his daughter's suitors in the story of Mergen. In contrast to Mergen, a responsible hunter who shows reverence for the sacred beings of Nature by helping the trapped deer, the power-hungry hunter Agamemnon becomes so possessed by killing that he destroys the very being he loves most.

Although he goes to battle in the name of civilized Greece against the Trojan barbarians, Agamemnon's own barbaric side possesses him, causing unnecessary bloodshed. He fights the Trojans to protect his brother's civilized marriage, but to do so he sacrifices his own humanity and "civility"—his duty to his own family and his daughter. Like Agamemnon, we all have within ourselves a domineering, barbaric, power-driven, warlike side that can mangle the innocent, trusting heart.

Mergen reminds me of the Even tribe hunters with whom I stayed in Siberia, for they understand that the deer will offer itself to them freely from the heart when the time is right. In contrast to Agamemnon's dishonoring of Artemis, thus trampling over the sacred deer quality in himself, the Even hunters pray in homage to the Reindeer Goddess before and after every hunt, recognizing her gift of the deer and respecting the holiness of her wild domain.

As portrayed in the Greek film version, *Iphigenia,* directed by Michael Cacoyannis, Iphigenia looks as lovely and as gentle as the sacred golden-antlered deer that Agamemnon slays. Iphigenia can be seen as a manifestation of the "wounded deer," the vulnerable feminine aspect of all women and men, a side of us that in wartime is sacrificed to greed and power. As a daughter, she is offspring, the hope for future generations. In killing her, Agamemnon is killing the hope of the future—gentleness and trust—qualities ascribed to the pregnant reindeer who journey for birth and the continuation of their species. The wounded deer, as depicted by Iphigenia in Greek drama and as shown through the dreams and experiences of the living women recorded in this chapter, is a tragic symbol for the sacrifice of the gentle feminine, our own civilized humane nature, and for the abuse of the greater Feminine, Nature, that has catapulted us into a dark time of social unrest and global devastation.

According to another legend, the ancient deer goddess, Artemis, saves Iphigenia at the last moment by secretly substituting a deer in her place during the sacrifice. Later, she appoints Iphigenia to be high priestess in her temple at Taurus. Perhaps, in demanding Iphigenia's sacrifice in exchange for raising the winds to sail, Artemis tricks Agamemnon, ultimately raising consciousness about war as a violation of the feminine spirit.

The shadow side of the deer woman is personified by Clytemnestra, who becomes a madwoman. Clytemnestra is furious that her own father has sacrificed her by giving her to Agamemnon in servitude to be a dutiful wife. She then swears revenge against her husband for sacrificing his own daughter to win back Helen, a symbol of the beautiful woman desired by men. Although, in this case, Clytemnestra uses the madwoman energy destructively when she murders Agamemnon in revenge, the tragedy in the story is so horrible that it provides an opportunity for those who hear it and understand it to become more conscious.

One of Artemis's trusts was to safeguard the independence of young girls. When young girls reached puberty, Artemis, as a virgin goddess, took them away to the woods in order to teach them to become aware, self-sufficient, and true to themselves before they were married. Through rituals in the forest, the deer goddess enlivened these young girls with the inner feeling of feminine freedom and centeredness, a sense of inner empowerment that can protect and heal the "wounded deer," much as the reindeer uses her antlers to protect herself and her newborn.

Ultimately, all of us who suffer from the injury to the wounded deer must learn how to use our antlers and to call upon the power of Artemis, the Deer Goddess, to stand up to those who would abuse us. In the following dream, Daphne, a woman who identifies with the wounded deer, uses this power to confront a hunter who has carelessly wounded a doe; he shows her the way to restore the deer to wholeness.

I am in the forest, standing in silent awe before the fragile beauty of a gentle doe. Suddenly there is a shot; the doe falls wounded to the ground, and a hunter emerges through the brush. Angrily I berate this man for carelessly wounding this beautiful being of nature.

The hunter is horrified at what he has done and hopes to heal the wounded doe. He tells me to fill a cup with the blood flowing from the wound and give it to the dying doe to drink. I am suspicious! This man has wounded the doe. Perhaps with these words he is trying to trick me into killing her. I hesitate when the doe suddenly speaks. She tells me that this ring of blood is nature's way of healing.

Daphne is a lovely woman with a receptive, open heart and gentle nature who had been wounded as a young girl by the rages of her alcoholic father. His unpredictable, drunken ranting frightened her and caused her to want to flee rather than to fight and assert herself. Later, as an adult, she was wounded by the collective patriarchal judgment against her sexual preference as a lesbian. Finally, she suffered when her natural intuitive and feeling manner and vision was put down as flighty and disparaged by teachers and supervisors as "soft-headed."

In the dream, Daphne is deeply aware of the doe's transcendent beauty. As she confronts the hunter and berates him for his cruelty, the hunter becomes conscious of his wrongdoing and wants to heal the wounded doe. While we may not always be able to change the hunter "out there" as

Daphne does in the dream, we can learn to talk to our inner hunter and transform him. With this change of consciousness, the wounded doe reveals the path to healing: to forgive the hunter by allowing him to participate in the cycle of healing. The flowing blood from the wound is the healing potion that the dying doe needs; it shows the rhythm of healing in nature and the continual round of death and rebirth. From the wound itself comes the solution for healing, just as suffering, when we accept and understand it, can offer us the heart's wisdom and compassion, the animal medicine of the deer.

In her own life, Daphne's transformation consisted in accepting her natural intuitive way and her tender heart as a strength rather than as a weakness. By confronting the hunter in her dream, she transformed the inner hunter that had wounded the deer and the outer hunter that had devalued her way of being. By accepting that she could heal the wounded doe if she listened to "doe wisdom," she began to experience self-esteem and to value herself as a whole person, including her sexual preference to be a lesbian.

The painful way in which many of us gain this wisdom is shown in the film *The Deer Hunter,* directed by Michael Cimino. The film depicts men and women living in a steel-mill community in Pennsylvania at the time of the Vietnam war. It focuses upon three steelworkers (Mike, Nick, and Steve) who have enlisted in the army to fight in the war, proud to go to Vietnam to serve their country. Accustomed to dangerous work at the blasting furnaces of the steel mill, the men drink and carouse in saloons to relax at the end of the day. The women's lives are centered on the men, who dominate them. The female protagonist, Linda (played by

Meryl Streep), is as gentle as the deer that the men eagerly hunt; she is a vulnerable, loving woman who is abused by her drunken father. Her girlfriends, too, are slapped around by their men, who blame them if another man happens to make a pass at them. Their difficult lives are like those of many women.

One weekend, a group of the men plan a hunting trip. By the time they reach the mountains, most of them have become drunk, loud, and obnoxious. Only Mike (played by Robert DeNiro) has respect for hunting and nature. Before the hunting trip he looks up at the sky and sees a formation near the sun, one that Native Americans regard as an omen for good hunting. When Mike draws the sun sign to their attention, the men laugh at him. Unequipped for hunting, lacking outdoor clothing, ill-mannered in their crude behavior, and unprepared in spirit because of their drunkenness and disrespect for nature, the men epitomize the unworthy, sinful, inept hunter that transgresses Artemis's holy forest.

Mike, the respectful hunter, is disgusted by their behavior. A deer, he tells them, must be taken by one shot to prevent needless suffering. For Mike, deer hunting is a spiritual venture. While the other men pollute the mountain sanctuary with their noise and boorish behavior, Mike leaves them and proceeds alone in the wilderness, hearing nature's transcendent music. As he shoots the deer that offers itself to him, he honors it. But after he returns with the deer, he joins the others as they go out drinking to celebrate at a saloon.

Before Mike, Nick, and Steve leave for Vietnam, they hold a wedding party for Steve, who must marry the woman he has made pregnant. The forced marriage is a sign of bad luck in the orthodox religion that they practice, but they abandon themselves to drinking and dancing nonetheless. At the restaurant where the party is under way, the men going to Vietnam are toasted. Everyone is high with drink and the excitement of the war. Noticing a Green Beret veteran at the bar, the enlisted men approach him with rash enthusiasm. His somber unresponsiveness puzzles them, but they soon forget as they continue to drink and party.

In Vietnam they discover that war is not the noble venture they had imagined. The violence is horrendous. Native villages are burned, and the people suffer agonizing deaths as their bodies are consumed by fire. American soldiers are killed, lose their limbs in combat, or are captured and tortured physically and mentally. Mike, Nick, and Steve are among those captured. One of the tortures they undergo is a game in which they are blindfolded and placed across from each other at a table. Their captors give each man a partly loaded gun to hold to his own head and order the blindfolded men to take turns pulling the trigger.

In this tortuous game of Russian roulette, Mike and Nick are forced to risk shooting each other as their drunken captors watch. While the torturers abandon themselves drunkenly to this brutal game, Mike realizes there is a chance to escape. In one of their lapses, he tricks and shoots the captors, so that he and Nick are able to escape. Rescuing Steve, whose leg has been injured and who is imprisoned in a swampy pit, the three men hide as they make their way down a river in the jungle. Under the pressure, Nick cracks and separates from Mike and Steve. Still struggling to try to save his injured friend, Mike is able to get Steve to a Red Cross truck. By the end of the war, Steve has lost his legs and become a cripple, while Nick, seized with madness as a result of the tortures and horrors he has witnessed, goes AWOL.

In America, the soldiers' friends await their return. Hearing that Mike is coming home with gold medals for his heroism, they hold a party in celebration for him. But Mike cannot go to the party. The war's atrocities have horrified and sobered him, like the Green Beret veteran he saw before he left.

Mike tries to return to normal life. He goes deer hunting with his old group of buddies. Again he leaves the other men and walks alone. As he walks through the forest hunting for the deer, Mike is moved anew by nature. Spotting the magnificent antlers of a great stag standing on the crest of a hill, he raises his gun. The deer looks him straight in the eye. Realizing the truth of the moment—that he can decide to kill the deer or not—Mike raises his gun above his head and fires in the air, choosing not to shoot the deer. Since he knows that his friends have not experienced the horror of war and will not understand his action, he tells them that the buck got away.

Later, noticing the head of a buck on the wall of a lodge, Mike recognizes that the stag's head is symbolic of his wounded buddies and a sign that he must try to find them. He hears that Steve has returned and tracks him down in a veteran's hospital. Now a paraplegic confined to a wheelchair, Steve hides in shame, saying, "I don't fit." But Mike convinces him to return to the community.

Before they went to Vietnam, Nick had asked Mike to promise that he wouldn't leave him there. Mike tries to fulfill that promise when he learns that Nick is still alive. Steve has received an anonymous package with money from Vietnam, and Mike knows that Nick has sent it to try to atone for abandoning his friend. Returning to Vietnam, Mike tracks Nick down in a gambling den. The gamblers repeat the torture they experienced in the war. Blindfolded, they sit opposite each other. Each holds a gun to his head in the game of Russian roulette, while the gambling bosses bet on who will live and who will die. Mike tries to get Nick to recognize him, but Nick spits in his face.

Desperate, Mike sits in the game opposite Nick, hoping to shock him into recognition by repeating the trauma they underwent as prisoners of war. Hoping to reach Nick, Mike holds the gun to his own head and pulls the trigger. He is lucky; he has drawn a blank. Mike mentions their common love of deer hunting, the mountains, and the trees that Nick once said gave him meaning. For a moment Nick seems to respond. Then, repeating Mike's words that a deer must be taken with one shot, Nick puts the gun to his head, pulls the trigger, and kills himself.

Mike returns to America with Nick's corpse. Sitting together after the funeral, the group of old friends, once naive and happy-go-lucky, now recognize the consequences of war. Nick, gone mad, has killed himself. Steve sits before them, a paraplegic. Linda knows their pain. Mike recognizes they are all like the deer. They can be free in spirit and as beautiful as the deer that run in the wilderness. But like the deer, they can be hunted down and wounded mercilessly as well.

The deer now serves Mike as a spirit guide. From the war, he has learned that those who kill can end up killing their human feelings. The challenge is to honor life. Despite the tragedy before them, Linda bravely and vulnerably starts to sing "God Bless America." The others join her singing humbly, aware of the dark side of their country. The rash arrogance of their prewar days has been transformed into humility before the mystery of life and death and before the paradox of good and evil.

Ultimately, the wounded deer is a metaphor for the human spirit, needlessly oppressed and abused. The brutality of war brings us all to this awareness. In the end, we are all wounded deer, and we are all the deer hunter as well. We have the choice to kill the deer, symbolic of the human heart's spirit of compassion. Or we can choose to allow it to run free.

In order to hunt, we don't necessarily have to kill. Rather, like Mike in *The Deer Hunter,* we can let the goal of hunting be to look into the eyes of the deer and meet it with compassion as a fellow being. Hunting in this way can be seen as an integral part of our transformation, since we all need to hunt for the heart's truth on our spiritual search for meaining.

Our lust for victory may show that we are more afraid of vulnerability and openness than we are of war. The temptation to wound, reject, or ridicule our vulnerability, embodied by the deer, threatens to injure our own aliveness and vitality. Wounding the deer disgraces the spirit of charity and mercy, the blessing of dignity, and thanksgiving for the gift of life. By stunting the spiritual potential of our deer qualities, we prevent ourselves from integrating this spirit into our lives. But if we respect our vulnerability and come to terms with it, and learn to follow the deer as a spirit guide, we can be led to transformation.

Nine

DOE WISDOM

n fairy tales as in dreams, a deer often guides the heroine or hero to an unexpected treasure, symbolic of a part of the psyche that we consciously need to integrate into our lives. Just as the reindeer doe finds the best place to cross rivers on actual migrations, so in fairy tales the hind shows the way of transformation. An Irish fairy tale, "The Enchanted Deer," tells of a young man's journey to follow a doe. By trusting the doe, he rescues the Deer Woman, thereby retrieving the spiritual wisdom of the mystical feminine; in a divine wedding he unites with his sacred soul mate.[1]

When Ian's father, a fisherman, is drowned at sea, Ian worries that he cannot provide for his mother and trades his horse for a hunting dog, a falcon, and a gun. He tells his mother what he has done, and she berates him for selling her property and beats him long and hard. Deciding not to take her abuse, Ian leaves home. He meets a farmer, who asks Ian to shoot a deer that has been eating up his corn. That night, Ian hides in the cornfield, sees the deer, and raises his gun to shoot. But instead of the deer, he sees a beautiful woman with long black hair standing where the deer had been. Blinking his eyes in surprise, he looks again and sees the deer. This happens three times; then the deer runs away. Ian decides to follow her.

After running a long time, the deer leaps onto the roof of a cottage and bids Ian to enter and eat. Soon twenty-four huge, mean-looking robbers return and find Ian in their house. Four of the robbers kill him. The next morning the deer enters the house, heals Ian, and restores him to life. The deer asks him to trust her and to stay there, promising him that no harm will befall him. Ian follows the deer's bidding, but the robbers return and kill him again, along with the four robbers who failed to kill him the night before. When the deer returns, she heals Ian again and asks him to stay another night. Ian stays and is killed once more by the robbers, who are so enraged that they fight and kill one another.

When the deer restores Ian to life a third time, she asks him to follow her to a cottage owned by an old woman and her dark, thin son. The deer says she will meet him the next day at a nearby church, then leaps across a stream and disappears into the woods. When Ian tries to meet the deer in the morning, he accidentally rubs against an enchanted "spike of hurt" that the old woman had hidden in the door crack. When the deer comes, Ian is asleep and she cannot awaken him. So she writes her name under his arm: "The daughter of the king of the town under the waves."

The second day at the cottage, Ian again tries to meet the

deer and again rubs against the spike and falls asleep. The deer woman comes but cannot awaken him. In tears, she combs his hair with a golden comb and places a beautiful box in his pocket. When she returns on the third day and finds Ian asleep, she sobs, for this was her last chance to have Ian break the spell that has been cast upon her. Sorrowfully, she returns to her home under the sea.

When Ian awakens, the thin, dark son taunts him that he will never see the tender deer woman again. But Ian knows he has been tricked, and he pledges to search the whole world for the beautiful deer woman. He travels so far that his shoes get holes and his feet grow sore. But he meets a kind woman who gives him ointment for his sores, invites him to eat and rest, and tells him to journey a year and a day to her sister. She gives him a pair of old shoes that will return to her when he reaches his destination.

Thanking her, Ian reaches the second sister, who helps him and directs him to the third sister, whose son is the keeper of the birds of the air and can help him. The bird keeper tells Ian to climb into a bag of red cow skin, which an eagle then carries to an island devoid of food. On the island, Ian, hungry, reaches into his pocket and finds the deer woman's box. When he opens the lid, three birds fly out and offer to help him. Ian asks the birds to take him to the kingdom under the waves where the deer woman dwells.

There Ian meets a weaver who tells him about a horse race; the winner will win the king's daughter for his bride. Ian calls the birds, who provide him with the finest horse and dress so that he can win the race. But instead of claiming his prize, Ian returns to thank the weaver. Ian wins two more races, leaves the prize unclaimed, and returns to the weaver's cottage in old dirty clothes. The king's messengers come in search of the race winner, but finding Ian in dirty clothes, they mistake him for an escaped thief and murderer.

The king orders that Ian be hanged on the gallows. As he mounts the steps to speak his last words, Ian raises his arm. The king's daughter sees her name written on his arm and realizes that he is the man who followed her and won the race, which breaks the spell upon her. She saves Ian and asks him how he found her. He mentions the birds in the box. Then the deer woman proclaims to the waiting crowd that she will wed Ian. Of all men, he alone trusted her and even sacrificed his head to be cut off three times for her sake. By trusting the deer, Ian freed her from the enchantment.

In this fairy tale, the tender feminine spirit, symbolized by the deer woman, is hidden deep in the unconscious—that is, in a kingdom under the sea. This suggests that feminine spirituality needs to be rescued, awakened, and brought to consciousness. Hidden feminine spirituality also appears in a Russian legend, where a young girl who is pure of faith prays to God to save their city, Kitesh, which is besieged by enemies. Answering her prayer, God preserves the city by hiding it in the depths of a great lake, where only the pure of heart can see it. To this day, the Russian peasants who dwell near the lake in Siberia believe that the spiritual people of Kitesh still live in the heavenly city under the water. Every winter, they walk out onto the frozen lake, kneel, and try to catch a glimpse of the celestial city and the woman of Kitesh.

The heroine of Kitesh at the bottom of the holy lake and the deer woman in the magical kingdom under the sea reveal to us the holy province of the mystical feminine, disparaged by many in our literal-minded culture, and offer us the opportunity to rediscover and retrieve it. Director Werner Herzog has recorded the peasants in Siberia who continue to search for the holy city in a film documentary. Anna Akhmatova has immortalized the legend in her poem, "The Way of All Earth"; Rimsky-Korsakov has eternalized it in his opera, "The Legend of the Invisible City of Kitesh."

In the Irish fairy tale, Ian represents the hero who can leave material things behind, see the enchanted woman in the form of the deer, follow her, trust her guidance, and sacrifice his head (rational thought) in order to save the deer woman, an embodiment of the mystical feminine spirit.

The fact that Ian's father was a fisherman who drowned suggests that the governing masculine aspect that pulls up fish—symbolic of information hidden to our awareness—has died and returned to unconsciousness. The mother, who beats Ian for selling her property, shows a dominant feminine side that is abusive, possessive, and materialistic. But the hero refuses to be treated without respect and leaves the domain of the abusive feminine to journey with his hunting equipment, just as we need to hunt for the tender feminine heart in ourselves, and retrieve and value it.

Had Ian chosen to shoot the deer for food for the farmer, he would have committed an act of aggression against the feminine—a typical reaction for a man who has had an abusive mother. But instead of resorting to violence, this hero has vision—he can see that the deer is a beautiful feminine being. Faithful to his vision, he follows the deer, who guides him to another challenge: to trust her and allow himself to be killed. By trusting her, he learns he can surrender and be healed and restored to new life. The murderous robbers kill themselves off, in the same way that we can shed our vicious resentments if we trust the transcendent forces symbolized by the deer woman.

The old woman who puts Ian to sleep with the "spike of hurt" represents revengeful, spiteful forces in ourselves that further regression and unconsciousness, that keep us hungry (her son is thin), and that work against being wakeful, as in the Buddhist practice of compassionate knowledge. The deer woman cannot awaken Ian directly, but she gives him a magic box with birds to help him to break the spell upon her. By writing her name under his arm, she gives him the means to find her. Her tears signify the watery realm in which she is hidden and connote the value that suffering can bring, in contrast to the abusive mother who resorts to rage.

By trusting the deer, Ian refuses to succumb to the thin, jeering dark son, who symbolizes the cynical, judgmental side of ourselves that tells us hope is lost and we were wrong. Instead, the hero breaks the spell of cynicism and revenge from the spike of hurt; he is conscious that falling into the sleep was not his fault but was due to a spell laid upon him. Children of abusive parents often experience spells of guilt for the abuse that has been put upon them. Their task, like the hero's, is to let go of the unnecessary guilt that is not their burden. Holding on to the burden of guilt usually continues the pattern of abuse—either as abuser or as victim. The hero of this fairy tale knows this is a trap, even though it may appear to be the easier way. Awareness of genuine responsibility requires the work of consciousness, which the hero chooses when he continues the journey.

Journeys toward consciousness are usually long and difficult, so lengthy that our feet may get tired and sore and our shoes wear down with holes. But if we keep to the journey, as Ian did, we find helpful feminine energies, such as the three sisters who feed him and give him a place to rest. Food is a recurring theme throughout the tale—Ian worries that he cannot provide food for his mother; the farmer asks him to shoot the deer for food; the deer woman offers him food in the robbers' cottage; the jeering son is thin; Ian is hungry on his journey; and the place to which the birds take him has no food. Like the cynical thin son, Ian has not received nurturing nourishment from his mother, and it is sparse in his environment. But by following the deer woman, listening to the sisters, and asking the birds for help, he finds the physical and spiritual nourishment that he needs.

The nurturing elder feminine aspect, symbolized by the sisters, directs him to the bird keeper, a helpful masculine side that is related to nature and protects the birds, symbolic of spiritual wisdom. The birdkeeper knows that every journey entails a Dark Night of the Soul, which is the meaning of Ian's being in the cow skin bag. The skin of the domestic cow contrasts with the wildness of the deer. Ian's journey in the bag corresponds to the night sea journey, the time of the Dark Night of the Soul when all we can do is surrender to nature's forces. Then we are helped by creatures like the eagle, which carries the bag to the island, and the birds in the magic box, which take him to the place where the deer woman dwells. If we surrender, we can come close to our natural instincts and heart.

This surrender reminds me of the sudden popularity of the twentieth-century Polish composer Henryk Goretsky, whose third symphony unexpectedly hit the top of the best-selling music charts thirty years after it was written. In this mystical meditative song, a sorrowing mother's lament over the death of her son transforms into affirmation as she surrenders him to the care of the birds and the flowers in the ground. Goretsky expresses in music the power of surrender. The popularity of Goretsky's symphony in our time suggests a collective need and desire for a mystical mediative way of being and a trust in nature that affirms even death.

Ian's meeting with the weaver who tells him about the race is like weaving the different threads of our own life quest so that we can find meaning. When Ian does not claim the prize right away but returns to the weaver, he shows the importance of giving thanks. Instead of taking the typical competitive way of claiming the prize and looking slick and successful, the hero demonstrates that he has the patience to wait for the right moment for the deer woman to recognize him, even in his dirtiest garb.

Although the king, the leading masculine principle in the fairy tale, mistakes Ian for a robber, the deer woman recognizes him as the man who has trusted her and even allowed his head (the rational intellect) to be cut off (sacrificed) out of love. By following the deer and trusting tenderness rather than rational calculation, Ian breaks the spell and the two can wed. In the same way, if we trust our hearts and follow our deer energy, we can break the spell of abuse and possessiveness in order to flourish in the divine wedding, the union with transcendent nature, symbolized by the wedding of the hero and the deer woman. By following doe wisdom, as Ian did, we can honor the mystical feminine spirit, trust its way, and revive and nourish the ancient feminine instinctual rhythm of soul that offers a path to the ecological, creative, and peaceful living needed by the modern world in its Dark Night.

The poet, Karl Kopp, who first referred me to "The Enchanted Deer," has expressed the elusive mystery of the deer that draws us to follow it in his poem, "Deer."

> How they fade   dissolve
> into deeper woods than these I own
> and clatter in

                (not quite true
for I go slowly slowly   a stick for snakes
through the leaf-mold   down the old logging
road
to the spring)
               Ah but they   how they move
into mystery

. . . .

they return   with a flirt of their tails
they are gone[2]

When deer look us in the eye and beckon us to follow them, whether in dream or in imagination as in the above poem, they embody an energy that wants to be seen and acknowledged. Usually deer lead the dreamer to a place of heart-vision where she sees something essential that she needs to integrate into her life. When a deer visits us in dream, imagination, and reality, she opens us up to her wisdom and can help us change our lives.

Caryn, a woman in a midlife crisis, told the following dream: "I was driving late at night alone on the highway. It was totally dark except for the headlights. Suddenly, to the right, I saw a deer standing and staring at me. I thought the deer was there for me. The deer's eyes were so gentle and kind. I knew this meant something important for me, but I had yet to figure out the meaning." Caryn tended to overwork, sometimes to the point of physical and emotional exhaustion. When she couldn't perform, she would be so critical of herself that she often fell into a depression so severe that she couldn't leave the house or get out of bed. The harsh, incapacitating self-criticism reflected the way her mother had treated her. For Caryn, the deer's kind and gentle look guided her to be compassionate and kind-hearted toward herself.

Looking into the eyes of a deer or following it is a dream motif for some women, like Caryn, who feel trapped in their lives. They see a deer entering their home, or they find it already inside. If they meet the deer's gaze when it looks into their eyes, it may lead them out from the house into the woods. Following a deer usually signals the start of a new phase in life.

Lisa, a professional in the healing arts, emphasizes the importance of following doe wisdom. During a bodywork session, at a time when she was trying to end a painful, unhealthy relationship, the image of a doe came to her. She was in love with a creative man who could not be faithful or commit to their relationship. In this imaginal experience, the doe looked into Lisa's eyes and beckoned to her to follow her into a forest and away from a field that was full of bucks. The doe motioned to her to lie down under an oak tree and covered her with thick, soft, moist moss and rich black earth. Then, the doe said, "Drink in the mother—let the mother heal you. You need to commit to stay in the forest and learn doe energy if you want to develop as a mature woman."

As the doe sipped water from a creek, she added, "Water is always flowing and will always be here." Upon hearing these wise words of the doe, who now had antlers, Lisa realized she could always drink of the doe's grace, strength, and emanating love. She recognized that she had been afraid to embody doe wisdom, since she feared her own gentleness and loving nature. She had confused gentleness with weakness and had chosen to adapt to buck energy. Following the doe, Lisa said, helped her to be true to herself and to change her tendency to betray her authentic self to please men.

The doe told Lisa that when she was a child, her mother had not known how to teach Lisa to be a woman, nor how to protect her from her father's abuse. Once her father came home drunk after a hunting trip and frightened Lisa by showing her a gutted doe he had killed; then he tried to force her to eat the meat. Horrified, Lisa refused. To punish Lisa, her father hung deer heads and antlers throughout the house. Such traumatic experiences had led Lisa to try to conciliate and adapt to dominating, seductive men. Inevitably, she betrayed her true feelings. After she followed the doe imaginally in the bodywork session and listened to her wisdom, Lisa was able consciously to integrate her natural gentleness with her innate strength and to develop into a mature woman with self-esteem.

Even to this day, the doe's image has stayed with Lisa, connecting her to the earth and to the divine union with nature that she experienced as a young girl. Remembering the doe, Lisa said, also helps her to connect naturally to people's feelings and instincts in her work as a movement therapist. When her father became terminally ill, Lisa was able to be with him, and to be patient and kind, and to forgive him. Her compassion enabled him to open up and ask her forgiveness just before he died.

Actual encounters with deer in nature bring many people the healing and wisdom they need. Emily had such an encounter when she was camping deep in the Appalachian Mountains, in a special place where her grandmother had taken her and where her mother and father had camped and courted. She wandered down a path to a creek, where she saw a lovely doe drinking from the water. The doe didn't run away but stood still and looked directly at her. Emily was struck with wonder because she had never before gazed into a wild animal's eyes. After the doe turned and walked away, Emily ran up the winding path to tell her friends; her heart was pounding, and the hair on the back of her neck prickled with excitement. As she ran, she saw the deer above her on a bluff, watching her.

This experience with the doe, Emily said, stayed with her as a source of strength, acceptance, and power. Twenty-two years later, during a time of personal crisis in which her father died, she was divorced, her job was in jeopardy, and a man whom she loved could not be with her due to tragic circumstances, a deer came into her life again to comfort her. On New Year's Eve, she was walking with friends at Point Reyes, California, nature reserve when she saw an elegant white doe standing by the trail. As soon as she saw the doe, her confidence in life was restored, and she felt the faith and trust that she would be all right.

Anna dreamed that she followed a deer that was traveling to give birth. Listening to the doe's wisdom connected Anna with her spiritual path as well as her unexplored cultural ancestry.

Deer is traveling through the woods when the urgency of birthing comes upon her. Drizzling rain dampens the earth, cleansing her space. The entrance to deer's sanctuary is a natural doorway, encircled by willows near a mountain stream. Deer enters and prepares a resting spot of moss from the nearby stream and fall leaves, all dried and crumbling, that are still composting the earth. Deer settles in—it is silent in the woods as the birth takes place with minimal effort and noise. There is no terror here with the birthing deer—only peace, love, and solitude as the new one is brought forth. I reflect for a moment on the hundreds of human births I have witnessed. One strikes out at me—Mona with the eyes of the deer and a gentle, noiseless birth—gentle birthing of spirit.

The mingling smells of blood, birthing fluids, and afterbirth permeate the willow grove. Mother deer walks to the creek for a refreshing cool drink after her energetic physical exercise to give birth. I see her with deer child, part human, and it's *me*. It was me being birthed with all the gentleness I could see in the doe's eyes that are full of tenderness toward me. Without words, I ask her, "Who am I?" and she replies, "You are your potential. You are here to walk the path up the mountain and will aid others up that path." I close my eyes and sleep the deep slumber of the newborn, part in and part out of this realm.

Later, during a workshop at a conference on shamanism and healing for women, Anna continued working with the dream by dialoguing with the deer in the following writing exercise. Using what Jung called active imagination, Anna could have a conscious exchange with dream material and retrieve more wisdom from the unconscious psyche.

I meet Deer and immediately we need to cross a wild river with a strong current to rejoin the rest of the herd. After we cross, I realize I cannot see where we had come from, but now we are in a grassy meadow with rolling hills around us and by a glacial lake. I ask Deer, "Can you help me understand my Dream?" She answers, "Will you follow me?" We meander along a trail around the lake until we come to a waterfall. We walk through it and she says, "Your tears made that waterfall."

We head toward a sacred temple of deer worship, a great pile of discarded antlers and a stone altar. I glance around at the surrounding rock cliffs and see pictographs of deer in red clay against the gray stone. The caretaker at the altar asks me to dance with Deer. He lifts a set of magnificent antlers onto my head and magically I dance. Then he gives me an amulet in the form of a deer made out of shiny stone and tells me to walk the Beauty Path just as the Deer walks that path. A message comes out of the stone altar into my hands: "You shall not kill. Deer are not predators. All living things must die in their own cycle, but not by your hands."

Anna hadn't known about the Sami people who actually follow the reindeer and long ago built stone altars called *seite*. At these sacred spots a reindeer doe was sacrificed to honor the Lady of the Reindeer, the hairy reindeer goddess who roams the mountains, leads the reindeer to green pastures, and protects mother and baby when the reindeer doe gives birth. Nor had she heard of Rozhanitsa, the reindeer goddess of the winter solstice, worshipped by the twelfth-century eastern Slavic peoples who believed that Rozhanitsa gave birth to humans as well as to deer.

For Anna, the doe's wisdom in the dream and learning about the birth-giving reindeer reaffirmed her spiritual direction and reunited her with her Slavic roots, a heritage whose meaning she had not yet explored. The dream also revealed the value of her tears, so powerful that they created a wondrous waterfall. It reinforced that gentle tenderness and peace are essential to the creative process through which we open to receive the wisdom and love needed to travel a spiritual path. When the caretaker of the deer temple placed antlers on her head, she felt linked to the shaman's ancient tradition to don antlers while performing their rituals.

To dance with Deer, to be given the deer amulet, and to be told to walk the Beauty Path are guiding principles that affirm doe wisdom. While Anna personally treasured this feminine way of being, she felt that Western culture belittled it. The final message—to honor Nature's cycle of life and death—is a spiritual guideline that she follows.

The secret of doe wisdom needs to be honored in our personal lives as well as in cultural life. If we do not incarnate this wisdom in our individual lives, we are less likely to be able to embody it in our families or in society. If we don't learn how to be gentle and compassionate with ourselves, how can we be kind to others?

Mother Teresa's life embodies doe wisdom—the profound insight and action of the humble heart that, like the doe in Anna's dream and the reindeer *vaja* in the Sami legend— vibrates with the music of creation's heartbeat. Mother Teresa once said: "There is a terrible hunger for love. God speaks from the silence of the heart." When Mother Teresa tenderly touches the forgotten people who are left alone— the sick and the poor—love pulses in her hands.

Just as we need to follow doe wisdom in our personal lives, we urgently need to revive it in contemporary culture. By following the deer, we can rescue and revive a gentle feminine instinctual rhythm of soul that many of us have lost in modern aggressive life. For the sake of global survival, we need to feel and venerate the mystical feminine spirit because, as history has shown, the conquerer's way leads to dangerous results that will destroy world life. Trusting the doe to guide us can lead us toward compassionate living and spacious existence that cuts across different generations, distant epochs, and diverse cultures. Opening our hearts, we can feel the common bonds that unite us so that we are able to honor and heal each other.

Etty Hillesum, a young Jewish woman who embodies the mystical feminine spirit in our century, wrote in her doe wisdom: "Mysticism must rest on crystal-clear honesty, can only come after things have been stripped down to their naked reality. . . . True peace will come only when every individual finds peace within himself; when we have all vanquished and transformed our hatred for our fellow beings of whatever race—even into love one day."[3] Etty was interned in Auschwitz when she wrote this. Despite all the atrocities she saw and to which she consciously bore witness, just before her death in Auschwitz she wrote: "things come and go in a deeper rhythm and people must be taught to listen to it, it is the most important thing we have to learn in this life. . . . The beat of my heart has grown deeper, more active and yet more peaceful, and it is as if I were all the time storing up inner riches."[4]

Once I had the privilege to be in Sikim at the Tibetan Buddhist monastery of His Holiness, the Karmapa Lama, whose life reverberated with the reindeer spirit. I was on an art history trip, and at that time, in the early 1970s, I had never heard of this man. In the year preceding this trip, however, I had had several dreams of Tibetan Buddhist temples, including one with striking imagery that I later saw painted on the wall of a secret chamber of his temple. As soon as I walked into the Karmapa's meditation room, I felt the supernatural energy of this gentle man. At his left, close to where he sat, was a glass door through which a weeping mother came to him with her little girl, who was four years old and suffering from a severe illness.

The Karmapa Lama stretched out his left hand to open the sliding glass door and gently touched the little girl's head. Healing rays of energy emanated throughout the room from his compassionate caress of the little girl and into all of our hearts. In this moment, we all felt blessed by his sacred touch, and I experienced viscerally the meaning of a Zen master's saying: "To be enlightened is to be intimate with all beings and to treat them as sacred." To me, the Karmapa's tender touch expresses the epiphany of doe wisdom and the reindeer *vaja*'s heart beating with love at the center of creation.

Ten

THE PATHFINDER

n ancient times, when people listened to the shamans' songs and to the rhythmic beat of their
magic drums, they were guided to follow the
Reindeer Spirit. In the Sami creation myth re-
counted in Chapter Three, the loving heart of the reindeer
doe is at the core of creation, and the shaman is the human
pathfinder. He or she directs the people in their understanding of the gentle feminine spirit and leads them to realize her
teaching, to respect the abundance of nature and appreciate
her gifts, and to see the truths of their lives and their unity
with nature. The shaman guides them in every aspect of their
lives. Like the reindeer, which the Sami follow on their
earthly migration, the shaman makes spiritual journeys as the
people's trailblazer to another world.

According to Mircea Eliade, the anthropologist and historian of religion who specialized in the study of shamanism, shamans journey in a trance state, during which the soul leaves the body and either ascends to the upper sky world or descends through the earth into the underworld. There they find spiritual power that they can bring back to earth to heal the wounds of a person or community. The shaman's journey is marked by ecstasy, and through it he or she creates new meaning and order from disharmony and chaos. As the great master of ecstasy, according to Eliade, the shaman is a visionary pathfinder to new ways of being that lead people into greater health, wisdom, and wholeness.

The shaman is "the great specialist in the human soul; he alone 'sees' it, for he knows its 'form' and its destiny."[1] While in their trance or altered state of consciousness, a shaman may radiate light to onlookers, who may see an aura or halo, like a colored crown, around his head. Although he is ecstatic, he is conscious and can see or hear spirits, feel his people's relationship to the supernatural world, and mediate between the two worlds. The shaman sees in the darkness and shows us the path, illuminating his visions for others. Shamans often work at night in the darkness of their tents, or in caves and underground caverns, or in the hollow of a tree. They make the classic Night Sea Journey for their people into the depths of the unconscious.

Before shamans make their journeys, they call upon the energies of their spirit animals to give them strength and to impart the qualities and power of the animal guide. Shamanic cultures believe in the primordial unity of animals and humans. They remember our basic human nature and our original kinship with animals. Contemporary and ancient shamans alike believe that they can transform themselves to embody the animal energy on their quest.

Through mimicking the animal and its sounds, wearing its mask, dramatizing its gestures, and dancing its movements to the beat of drumming and rattling, which helps bring the altered state, the shaman becomes one with the animal and gains insights into its untamed nature and energies. She can later reveal to the human community how it can integrate the animal energies. This conscious, active metamorphosis into the spirit animal requires the shaman to release her ordinary ego consciousness, which may have an ecstatic aspect but which is also often psychologically painful because of the loss of identity. Sometimes experienced as a dismemberment, this loss of identity is a symbolic death that enables rebirth. It may be a part of the shaman's initiation as healer.[2]

Many Siberian shamans perform a reindeer dance. Typically, a woman shaman, wearing a dress of reindeer fur and hide, dons reindeer antlers and mask and pendants that sound like the clatter of reindeer hooves. She adapts the animal's movements and sounds and chants songs in praise of the holy celestial reindeer, then sits astride her drum, made of tree trunk wood and reindeer skin. The drum becomes the reindeer that she rides on her journey. At the same time the shaman "becomes" a reindeer herself and goes into an ecstatic state, in which she spontaneously seems to spring like a reindeer. If she is trying to heal a sick or dispirited person and recover their soul from the evil spirit that has caused the stress, her reindeer spirit will fight with the evil spirit. If the evil spirit wins the contest, the patient may die. In these cases the shaman returns with lowered head, and her drum sounds dull. But if the shaman's reindeer wins the battle with the evil spirit, then the patient recovers and the shaman returns in good humor.[3]

A contemporary Nganasan shaman from Siberia, Tubiakou, describes his shamanic ritual.[4] He wears a parka made of reindeer suede, with a chain sewn on the shirt's back. The chain allows his helpers to pull him back from the treacherous journey to the other world when he is in a deep trance. Carved bone, copper, and iron figures are sewn on the front of his costume to protect his belly. The iron geese he wears are meant to assist his magical flights by directing the elements of air, earth, and water. He wears a bear claw bracelet on his wrist, and on his skull is a headband with iron antlers, meant to be those of the Heavenly Deer. Hanging suede strips hide his eyes, protecting others from the gaze of the potent spirits that enter him during the rite. Upon his traditional frame drum, symbols, including reindeer, are painted. Soft fur from the deer's legs covers the mammoth-bone clapper.

The Nganasans, who believe they are descended from reindeer, make a drum that they perceive as a reindeer itself. Its four legs, made of four forged iron staples, hold the stretched skin of a wild reindeer. Teeth shapes, made of beads, are sewn into the deerskin. Tubiakou has twenty-one spirits to help him, and he drums to acknowledge their presence and ask for their aid.

To begin his mystical flight, he sings a song honoring the reindeer doe—it was taught to him by a divine force that he calls God's Mother. He sings the same song to end the ritual. During his flight, he travels between the spread legs of the upper world goddess, the World Female, the primordial being.

Tubiakou, who can communicate with spirits from the three upper, middle, and lower realms, believes that God's Mother places a special soul into a shaman, which calls him to undergo a long, arduous, and painful process until he becomes worthy of the supernatural powers given to him. He may be called on to fast, live as a hermit, suffer from illness or madness, or endure excruciating initiatory tests. In all these trials he proves his strength. Evil spirits may try to prevent his earthly return and the restoration of the soul he is seeking. The shaman also performs four seasonal rituals, including the vernal equinox ritual, in which the *chum* (special dwelling) is purified and the spirits are asked to protect the reindeer from wolves and to provide good hunting. A shaman who fails in these trials or ignores performing the rituals may be punished with declining powers, illness, or depression.

Tubiakou reports that he once neglected to perform one of the annual seasonal rituals. He believes his wife became ill as a result of this failure. He was unable to save her life and she died. Like Job in the Old Testament, Tubiakou lost his faith after her death. He suffered a depression during which he abandoned all of his shamanic responsibilities, and he even sold his ritual costume to a museum. Later, realizing he could not escape from his calling, he surrendered to his shamanic vocation once more.

The following dream was told me by Jason, a contemporary healer, a psychotherapist. At the time of this dream, Jason was not yet a therapist but was in search of his own soul and at the brink of a crucial life transformation. The dream shows an initiate called to the path of individuation and healing through shamanic vision.

The scene is a forest. There is a great tree that has opened up to reveal a chamber inside. A woman, Katharine Hepburn, has decided to wait for the arrival of the warrior. He comes—a kind of reindeer shaman wearing antlers on his head. He approaches—gives her a feather and a robe ceremonially—lifts her hand to his mouth

slowly—then his face changes—flushes, his eyes grow
fierce, he opens his mouth, snarls and tears a piece of
flesh from the woman's forearm and eats it. The woman
is startled, clearly in pain, but is transfixed.

This dream was so powerful that Jason drew a picture of it
after he awoke. In his early thirties at this time, he was learning to relate to his feminine soul. In the dream Katharine
Hepburn represented a strong independent woman, one in-
telligent and capable of relationship, a wise woman who
would be very attractive to him as a friend, he said.

The hollow of the great tree is a typical place for the
beginning of a shamanic journey. In the context of shamanism, the tree is the World Tree, the cosmic tree of life, the
world axis, which unites the upper spirit world, the middle
earthly world, and the lower underworld—the three realms
in which any initiate must learn to travel. As Jung pointed
out, the shaman in all of us must learn to climb the cosmic
tree in order to find the true self in the upper world. This
entails a mystical experience in which the initiate receives
direct knowledge and a felt vision about the other reality—
knowledge that comes from the heart and is not merely intel-
lectual.

Jason was a compassionate man on a spiritual path, a man
with heart. Developing his inner spiritual warrior, in the
form of the reindeer shaman, was a necessary part of his
development. In the dream, tearing the piece of flesh from
the woman's forearm is analogous to the phase of dismemberment in a shaman's initiation—the conscious experience
and acceptance of pain and suffering that can lead the initiate
to rebirth and rapture and to the knowledge of human
wounds. A shaman, or any person, must accept her own

wounds in order to become a "wounded healer," who from the process of healing herself has learned the path for healing others. The shamanic calling is frequently revealed in a big dream, such as the above dream, and in the case of Jason, it presaged his future vocation as a psychotherapist.

The film *Pathfinder,* set in the vast winter wilderness of Lapland and based on a thousand-year-old Sami legend, shows the initiation of a young boy who is called to be a shaman for his people. It also depicts abuse of the gentle feminine, symbolized by warlike invaders who kill his sister and try to destroy the peaceful Sami people.

Directed by Nils Gaup, the film is the first in the Sami language and presents an authentic picture of Sami shamanism and Sami lifeways. At the film's start, the viewer sees a mysterious vision that the shaman Raste has seen only three times in his life—once in his youth, once in midlife, and once just before his death—a vision of the majestic and mystical white reindeer. Raste knows this vision portends a significant event for his people.

Aigin, a sixteen-year-old Sami boy, is returning home on his skis from hunting. In his absence, a band of plundering warriors, the Tchudes, find his family and slay them. First the marauders, dressed in black metallic armor, shoot his family's dog with a crossbow; then they shoot Aigin's young sister and finally his parents. Aigin arrives at the crest of a nearby hill just in time to witness the Tchude invaders putting the bloody corpses of his parents and sister into a hole in the snow and pillaging his home.

Aigin flees to try to warn the other Sami people. But the Tchude warriors see him, wound his arm with a crossbow, and follow him to try to kill him. The wounded Aigin travels miles, leaving a trail of blood through the snowy wilderness, and collapses just as he reaches a Sami settlement. When he awakens, he warns the Samis that they must stay and fight the fierce marauders. But most of the peace-loving Sami feel they are no match for these cold-blooded killers, whom they regard as the essence of evil. Most of the men, women, and children flee by reindeer-drawn sledge to warn the people of another Sami community who live two days' distance away.

Meanwhile Aigin, deep in despair over the death of his family and the horror he has witnessed, remains in one of the tents to recover from his wound. A young girl about his own age, Sahve, tends him. She feels his despair, but she intuits his potential goodness and heroism and communicates her admiration to him before she leaves with the rest of the people. Later, Raste the shaman visits him.

Aigin senses the wisdom of the shaman, but his despair overwhelms him. Telling the shaman that he has lost all faith and meaning, Aigin confesses his hopelessness and bitterness. Raste knows that his words alone will mean nothing to Aigin in this crisis, so he asks Aigin if he can see anything of value. Looking around the empty tent, Aigin replies that he sees nothing at all. The shaman asks Aigin the question once more, and the boy replies again that he sees nothing. Suddenly, the shaman grabs the boy from behind, puts his hand over his mouth, and cuts off his breath.

After a long moment, Raste releases the gasping boy, who is shocked by the shaman's action. Then Raste tells him that the common air that they breathe to stay alive unites people. The Sami people know they are related, Raste says. That is why they can live in harmony and peace and help each other. But the Tchudes, by forgetting the vital knowledge of human relationship, have lost this unity. They have cut themselves off from humanity and from one another. This will be their downfall, the shaman predicts.

Understanding the truth the shaman has given him and remembering the love he saw in Sahve's eyes, Aigin pulls himself together and commits himself to life once more. At that moment, Raste shares with Aigin his visions of the white reindeer. Aigin's experiences are the beginning of his initiation as a shaman, a vocation that the older shaman recognizes in the boy.

Soon the invading Tchudes reach the camp, and Raste, foretelling that his own death is near, hands his magic drum to Aigin to hide inside his parka in order to keep it safe. He instructs Aigin to give it to the wise elder woman of the tribe as soon as he reaches them. Just then, the armed Tchudes capture Aigin and Raste and demand to be led to the rest of the Samis. Wounding Raste severely, the Tchudes threaten to kill him. Alarmed, Aigin tells the Tchude warriors that he will lead them to the Samis if they spare Raste's life.

Forced to lead the evil Tchudes to slaughter his people, Aigin bargains for time. He takes them the short way, over a treacherous pass that corresponds to the holy mountain, Passevaari, a route that only Sami people know. As they reach the mountaintop, he notices that one of the Tchudes has the knife that Aigin had slipped to Raste to protect himself—that the knife is in the Tchude's possession means that Raste has been killed. Aigin conceives an ingenious plan. He tells the Tchudes that in order to maneuver the treacherous pass successfully, they will have to tie themselves together. Only he knows the way, and the Tchudes are dependent on him to get through the pass.

With Aigin at the lead, they tie themselves to a rope to cross the pass and descend through the abyss below. At a crucial moment, Aigin suddenly jumps over the edge. He grabs on to a boulder, but the Tchudes fall down the mountain. Not united to his fellows by any value, each Tchude cuts the rope to save his own life. Cutting themselves apart is their downfall, as Raste had predicted and told Aigin in the tent. The Tchudes' frantic movements to save themselves set off an avalanche in which all the killers fall to their death. Having tricked the Tchudes to their own death without using violence himself, and in awe of Nature's ferocity in the avalanche that has saved the Samis from the Tchudes, Aigin starts to descend the mountain. As he looks up at the peak of the holy Passevaari mountain, he has a vision.

A great white reindeer appears suddenly from the mist, looks Aigin powerfully in the eye, then disappears back into the moving clouds from where he came. Although Aigin is not yet aware of the vision's meaning, it confirms his destiny as a shaman. Finally he reaches the Sami settlement and explains what has happened. He tells them that they are safe, but that Raste is dead. Then he hands the shaman's drum to the elder woman. "We have lost our pathfinder," the people lament when they hear of Raste's death. But the elder woman, in her wisdom, knows better. "We will *always* have a pathfinder," she says. Looking into Aigin's eyes, she gives the newly initiated shaman the Samis' magic drum.

In the film the round smiling faces of the Sami people, framed by the soft fur of their reindeer parkas, contrast with the dark, mean look of the Tchudes, who wear hard steel armor. The Samis value spontaneity and playfulness; in a scene in a sauna, the naked women laugh with one another as they bathe, and they tease a good-natured Sami man who accidentally walks in on them. In their culture, vulnerability is a virtue and does not conflict with hard work and the capacity to survive in the harsh Arctic wilderness. They accept Nature's ways—its generosity and its ferocity—and try to live in harmony within its bounds. Following Nature is their path.

By contrast, the gigantic Tchude men, dressed in metallic black armor, represent the cruel, heartless, oppressive forces of life out of balance. Shooting the dog symbolizes the wounding and murder of our animal instincts and our connection with nature by the greedy cold-blooded power-driven side that kills without regard for life and abrogates the priceless qualities of vulnerability and gentleness. The murder of Aigin's sister represents slaying the spirit of the gentle feminine side in all of us.

The actions of the aggressive Tchudes, as portrayed in the film, parallel those of the patriarchs of the Christian Church, who in 1700 actually tried to destroy Sami shamanism by taking away their ritual drums. Just so, the Stalinists in Siberia tried to eradicate the practices of the Even and other shamanic peoples of Siberia. Still today, in our society, rationalists try to disparage mystics and other people who have nonrational spiritual approaches to life. Although many contemporary people have shamanic dreams with redemptive visions, they often live under the domination of people like the Tchudes. The loss of the wisdom of shamanism in our modern world is a serious spiritual problem, and the search to reclaim nonrational modes of knowing is the spiritual quest of our times.

The dream of Marla, a contemporary woman, shows the instinctive impulse that many people have to return to the healing way of the shaman; and it shows how difficult it can be to follow this path. Marla's dream, which takes place in a traditional shamanic setting, reveals the dilemma that faces many women and men whose natural shamanic gifts conflict with Western patriarchal organized religions. The dream also emphasizes healing from the feminine spirit.

I am in an underground cavern, searching, waiting for a vision or a sound or something. Off to the side, a woman sits in a dim light beating a drum. While walking around in the darkness, there is chaos and people begin to crowd around me. I am uncomfortable and anxious. All of a sudden there is a note in my hand on carbon paper. It is difficult to read and I can only decipher the words "be careful" and something about a Bible. Afraid, I begin looking for a Bible. Just then a man furtively hands me a Bible he had hidden in a pouch around his waist. I am frightened and I do not want it.

I run out of the dark underground cavern upstairs into a brightly lit room where a group of men are standing around. First, I pass an Episcopalian priest. Next I walk by a famous thinker. Then I see a well-known Jungian writer. As I walk toward him, I call out the name of a contemporary shaman, who hugs me to him and whispers in my ear, "Do you know Yahweh?" As I try to figure out who Yahweh really is, the shaman says, "Never mind," and touches my neck below my ear.

My head is filled with a ringing sound, and I am transported to another place. I wake up, still in the dream, in front of a reddish-brown cave wall. A huge bearskin hangs on the right side of the wall. To the left, above the bearskin, are petroglyphs of reindeer; at the bottom is a feline, probably a panther. The reindeer petroglyphs begin to move back and forth on the wall. Watching the dancing reindeer in fascination, I awaken.

Marla's dream is a striking portrait, not only of her own predicament but of that of many other modern women as well. As a child, she had been raised in a patriarchal form of Christianity that had become dry and lifeless. The significance of her own mystical feminine vision had been subtly diminished. Now shamanism seemed a viable spiritual path, more akin to Marla's own nature. The woman drumming in the cave in her dream symbolizes this shamanic side of herself. The man, who distracts her with the unwanted Bible, represents the Christian patriarchy to which Marla was still partially attached.

Passing by the minister and the thinker—also representatives of the patriarchy—she heads toward the Jungian writer, a man who is known for his appreciation of the feminine. As she approaches him, he becomes a man known for his shamanic sight. By asking her who Yahweh is, then saying, "Never mind," the shaman helps her to move away from Yahweh, the primordial, capricious, punishing Old Testament God, back to her own direct feminine spirituality and shamanic knowing, represented by the ancient animal symbols in the cave. She needs to "know" Yahweh in order to avoid being caught in that religious system.

Marla told me that the dream signified the wedding of the ancient masculine and the ancient feminine. Going back to the cave was an attempt to find the deeper religious spirit for which she was searching, to return to her direct feminine way of knowing, symbolized by the gentle dancing reindeer and the powerful panther.

The ringing sound that she hears when the shaman asks

her about Yahweh and the feeling of being transported to another place—the cave—are typical elements of a shamanic journey. The bearskin and the petroglyphs of the panther and reindeer present her with animal powers that she can embody in her life. The dancing reindeer that draw her attention are calling her to partake of their special energy.

By sharing our significant dreams, our stories, and those of other cultures, we can reassert the spirit of shamanism in ourselves and in our society. Shamanism, or the spirit it evokes, is of great importance in modern times because we have lost our sense of the spiritual path. In order to find it, we must first recognize the inner (and often the outer) path-finder that emerges in the psyche whenever an individual is ready, knowingly or not, to take the path.

In *The Way of the Shaman,* anthropologist Michael Harner points out that when an animal guide emerges from the psyche, the embodiment of its spirit is purely beneficial. The animal spirit, he says, needs to be "exercised, not exorcised." Exercising means inviting and evoking an animal's spirit by calling the beast to oneself and dancing with the animal, singing its songs, and recognizing its appearance in significant dreams or through a solitary vision quest. Running with the animal in a wild place is another way to exercise its power. As in all transformation, a consciously committed, routine practice is necessary to integrate the new energy.[5]

Sometimes we can recover and adopt an essential energy by learning how shamanic peoples live. This was one reason that Keith and I traveled to so many northern countries. We wanted to see their practices firsthand and see if we could physically and spiritually accomplish them in a way that pre-served their integrity. So our hosts guided us in their own way of life, governed by their worldview. When Keith and I actually rode a reindeer, for example, the elder cautioned us not to extend our hands too near the deer's antlers, which hold the holy power of the world tree. Sami poems and songs also reflect the spiritual connection between antlers and branches.[6]

Among the Even, too, we found lifeways and practices that embody this essential energy. The Even honor death, and they believe that their dead friends will continue to ride the reindeer, as do all those who have made the journey before them. They celebrate new life every June on the summer solstice, the beginning of their New Year, which commemorates the renewal of nature. Green grass abounds in the lush mountain valleys at this time, one month after the new reindeer are born in May. June, "the blossoming month," is named after the newborn reindeer, the blooming flowers, and the redolent herbs. In the summer solstice ceremony, everyone rejoices, sings songs, dances, and plays. The men look for brides and compete to show their strength. Every woman, man, and child dances in the grand circle toward the direction of the sun to acknowledge that they are the sun's children and are about to take the sacred journey to the sun. The great dance circle shows the endless circle of time without beginning or end.

On the morning of the summer solstice, the Even perform a rite to welcome the sun. They arise early in the morning to meet the sun's rays in the beautiful open valley. Then they tie colorful ribbons to a rope stretched between two trees. Each ribbon represents a separate family in the community. They make two fires, and everyone is silent as they wait for the sun to rise and shine through the tree gate, which faces the sun. When the sun appears, each person steps over the first fire to purify themselves, then faces the sun, prays, and asks for health for themselves, their community, and the reindeer in the new year.

Living an ancient legend, they step over the second fire while riding the spirit reindeer, which carries them through the sky to the sun. After they reach the heavenly divinity, who promises them good luck, they return on the reindeer's back, then take the saddles from the sacred deer's backs, as though returning from a long journey. All this is done in mime, an enactment of their seasonal prayer in which they follow the path to the sun and reconnect the people to the inner pathfinder. After the ritual journey, they eat, then dance in the great circle as children of the sun. When the shamans were still alive, the elder said, they consecrated this holy place before and afterward.

Although all their shamans had been murdered during Stalin's reign of terror, the elder said, the people still continue to live a shamanic way of life by honoring the earth, the sun, and the reindeer each day, and by performing rituals. At the International Siberian Shaman Conference that we attended in Yakutsk, just after our visit to the Even people, scholars of ethnography, anthropology, and the history of religion all told us that in the last two years after perestroika, new shamans were beginning to identify themselves in Siberia. Hope for the future lies in shamanism, one after another of the conference speakers agreed, for shamanism offers the possibility of universal spirituality and freedom. It is grounded in our common experience of nature's transcendence and the unity we share with all that is. Honoring this experience of awe and joy gives spiritual meaning to our individual and collective lives.[7]

Even in these dark times of ecological and personal despair, we still have a choice. We can become identified with the plundering Tchudes, whose greed and negation of the unity of all living beings destroys human life and the earth on which we live. We can indulge ourselves in despair, as Tubiakou did during the time when he lost faith and abandoned his shamanic calling. Or we can be like the Sami people, portrayed in the *Pathfinder,* and like the Even people of Siberia—hardy yet heart-full survivors, cooperating generously with one another, moving together with Nature and not against it. And always, always grateful to be on the journey that is guided by the spirit and the loving, healing heart of the reindeer doe that beats in the World's Dark Night like the beat of the shaman's drum.

Eleven

THE REINDEER
PEOPLE

he Far North is a mysterious land that fascinates
and frightens us, for little there is predictable or
familiar. The Reindeer People who inhabit this
region know the extremes of their land's conditions as well as those of the human condition, which most of
us experience with lesser intensity. Theirs is a life based on
survival in an environment that can be lethal, uncompromis-
ing, severe, and relentless. At other times, it can be bountiful.
Thus, the Reindeer People live in perpetual paradox. They
learn to endure tensions of opposites, for they live with
beauty and terror, success and downfall, feast and famine,
celebration and defeat, delight and horror. At every moment
the Reindeer People live face-to-face with life and death.

Survival is paramount to all of us, and Arctic peoples,

vitally alert to the stark realities of the struggle for existence, provide us with an example of how to survive in extreme conditions in a peaceful way. Eminently practical, they are also deeply spiritual, for they are aware of the holiness that is immanent in ordinary life. The Reindeer People exemplify the inherent unity of the mystical and practical aspects of life. The Siberian tribes, for instance, believe that everything that moves is alive and that a spirit dwells in every living thing. All living beings, they believe, share a spiritual kinship that stems from a common origin. As a Chukchi shaman explained to anthropologist Waldemar Bogoras: "All that exists lives. The lamp walks around. The walls of the house have voices of their own. Even the chamber-vessel has a separate land and house. The skins sleeping in the bags talk at night. The antlers lying on the tombs arise at night and walk in procession around the mounds, while the deceased get up and visit the living."[1] All of life, including death, is sacred, and the task for humans is to bear witness to the world's wonders through an attitude of respect, reverence, and awe.

Attitudes toward the hunt and its practices reflect the sacredness of life to the nomadic peoples of the Arctic. Since hunting animals is their primary means of survival, they try to foster trust and reciprocity with the animals they hunt. Reindeer gave the early nomadic peoples everything they needed for survival. The inland tribes ate reindeer meat for their basic diet. They used the reindeer's hide to make clothing, roof coverings for their tents, bedding, footwear, cooking wares, and canoes. They rode the reindeer to hunt and used them to carry their mobile homes. When necessary, they bartered reindeer for other products.

The Naskapi Indians from the Labrador peninsula believe that humans and animals differ only in outward form. Inwardly, animals and humans are identical, sharing a spiritual existence that transcends physical differences and that unites them after death. They revere animal life as much as human life. Killing an animal must be carried out only according to ethical principles. If a hunter and an animal meet, it is to fulfill each other's destiny. If the hunter kills the animal, he shows respect. For example, it was a Naskapi practice to put the animal's bones, such as the caribou's shoulder blade, in a sacred place. The bones were then used in the rites of divination.

For the aboriginal Arctic peoples, as for most aboriginal peoples, animals mirror the human soul, forming the basis for empathy and compassion between humans and their animal friends. A good hunter knows that success in killing a deer, for example, is due not only to his own skill but to the deer's generosity in giving itself, in order that the people who depend on it for food may live. Thus responsible hunters of many tribes—the Samis in Lapland, the Even in Siberia, the Crees in Canada, to name only a few—share common spiritual and moral values in relation to the animals they hunt. They use every part of the animal, wasting nothing. They respect the animal's soul and body by ritually following the proper way to retrieve the animal, butcher it, eat it, and dispose of its bones. It is essential to avoid causing the animal undue distress, they believe, by killing it as quickly and painlessly as possible. Only enough animals to survive are killed; killing is never for sport or ego exaltation.

When a hunter kills an animal, the meat belongs to the entire tribe and is shared by all members of the community, including guests. Sharing with everyone present is a prime value of the Even, a tradition they call *nimet*. According to this tradition, the hunter who kills an animal offers it to the other hunters as their gift. When Keith and I were guests of the Even in Siberia, we were offered everything that the tribe members ate. A rib of meat was passed around the campfire, along with a knife, and each person cut off as much or as little as they wanted. In this way, nothing was wasted—a sharp contrast to the excessive amounts of food with which we were inundated in Russian hotels. We felt sad and guilty that we could not eat all the food, for we knew that many Russian people were starving outside our hotel doors.

During meals with the Even, the women poured into our cups holy milk that they had extracted that day with reverent care from the sacred udders of the reindeer doe. At the end of our stay, the elder invited us to share with the entire tribe the blessed blood of a reindeer they had just sacrificed. We drank the fresh warm blood in celebration with the reindeer people, aware that this was one of their greatest gifts to us, yet knowing that our refusal would also have been accepted. The Even elder had already told us that they honor the different ways of other peoples of the earth.

One of their oft-told stories, "Stingy Reindeer Owners," emphasizes Even moral teaching.[2] One winter, when the days were very short, some people gathered to live near each other. All were wealthy reindeer owners, except for an old shaman who had nothing to eat. Although they had plenty of food, the wealthy people did not offer the old man a single thing to eat, so the elder shaman went to bed hungry. That night he had a dream. When he awoke, he told the best hunter in his own family that the family should move, for in his dream, wolves had come and driven away all of the reindeer. The old shaman's family moved away, but the richest people, who had never been hungry, paid no attention to the shaman. They could see their herd right there near the camp. Instead of listening to him, they played cards, laughed, and were noisy.

The next morning, mysteriously, all of the reindeer, even

the very deer that the people rode, had disappeared. Only wolves' tracks could be seen in the snow. The rich family had nothing left and had to stay in camp while a brutal snow storm raged for days. The people became so hungry that they ate their saddles, the tent coverings, and even their own clothes. Now naked and cold, they had no food for ten days and even started to chomp at their hands. When the storm finally stopped, a rich man in the family left to try to find food. After a day of fruitless searching, when he could walk no longer, he stopped in the middle of the desert, crying aloud in despair. Suddenly, from under the ground, a stranger appeared. It was the Master of the Desert. He told the rich man not to cry and said that, he, too, was an owner of reindeer.

The extraordinary stranger told the rich man that he would give his family something to eat, provided they remembered the ancient Lamut custom: to give the best morsel of food to a poor neighbor. The rich man agreed. After he returned home the next morning, a huge herd of gray wild reindeer unexpectedly appeared near their camp. The people could see that the largest animals had been ridden, for their backs showed the wear of saddles. In actuality, they were the special riding reindeer of the Master of the Desert.

The family lived off the reindeer the rest of that winter, and when spring came, they moved with the herd and pitched their tents near some other people. In the new camp lived some poor people who were very hungry. The rich man and his wife decided not to feed these good-for-nothing people but to move on instead. So the rich family left the camp and pitched their tents alone. When they awoke the next morning, they saw that all of the reindeer that had come to them so unexpectedly had disappeared as suddenly. Only their tracks remained in the ground. Angry with these hard-hearted people who had not learned how to share despite his great gift to them, the Master of the Desert had ordered his reindeer to fly away into the heavens. When the rich family returned to the camp they had just left and asked for some food, they were told that since they had given nothing before, they would receive nothing now. In the end, the rich family starved to death.

This tale is only one of many Siberian stories that reflect the strong moral values necessary for human survival, as well as the mysterious gift of the transcendent reindeer that can appear so suddenly and disappear in the same uncanny way. Like the rich man and his family, we, too, often do not value what we have, much less immaterial gifts such as the ineffable reindeer. Neither, like the rich family, are we always aware of the importance of our connection to others, or of the ways in which our own lives depend upon our community, our environment, and its nonhuman inhabitants. Yet "modern" as we may be, we are all as "dependent" and as "independent" as the Reindeer People. For our lives too hinge upon food, shelter, reproduction, animals, the fruitfulness of the earth, and the ecocycle, as well as the human community.

In the Arctic cultures an animal that offers itself to the hunter is regarded as a guest who has offered a gift of his own accord. When slain, the animal is thanked, praised, and asked to come again in another form. Usually the thanks and praise are given in a ritual sacrifice. The Arctic people believe that the animal's soul will return to earth, a belief similar to the ancient Sami conviction that the white reindeer is a reborn soul.

Siberian folk tales often relate that certain animals formerly were human beings and vice versa. For example, the Bering

Sea Eskimos believe that the caribou, like all other animals, has a soul *(yua)* in human form. Sometimes the caribou's soul reveals itself through human speech.[3] Some stories tell of the intermarriage of humans and beasts. The offspring of such marriages often inherit the union of animal energy with human intelligence. Originally, the kinship between humans and animals was experienced as familial. Hence the people might refer to an animal as a sister, a brother, or a grandmother. Within this framework, humans differ from animals in outer appearance but not in their inner basic nature. Animals are the great teachers from whom human beings learn substantially about their own nature and their inner powers. This idea of animal teachers is found in our own Western fairy tales, too.

In Arctic cultures, the seamstress who transformed the reindeer's skin into clothing for humans knew that she was reconciling humans and animals through the clothing. She believed that a reindeer skin dress maintained its animal identity and served as a second skin for the human being who wore it. The animals, hunters, and seamstresses were linked spiritually, and the transformational relationship between animals and humans was embodied in the very clothes that the seamstress made and that the people wore. For instance, the Chukchis believed that "skins ready for sale have a 'master' of their own. In the nighttime they turn into reindeer and walk to and fro." They believed that the amulets made from animals also could change into the original animal if necessary.[4]

By imitating an animal—mimicking its behavior, dancing its movements, singing with its voice, making and wearing a face mask of the animal—or by carving or painting its image, the people communicated with the animal in ritual tribute. In this way, they paid respect and gained access to the animal's energy, which corresponded to a part of themselves.

They also honored the animals by giving their children animal names. The paths and places where a certain animal passed often bore its name. The people understood animals, empathized with them, talked to them, and were grateful for their presence. To insult an animal, to be cruel or even indifferent to it, was considered a grave offense with serious consequences, as in the story of "The Woman Who Put a Bucket Over the Caribou's Head."[5]

In this Point Barrow Eskimo story, a man is known for his skill in hunting on both land and sea. Always he hunts only what he needs, and whenever he brings back a caribou or seal to his wife, she treats it properly, with due respect. She gives water to the sea animals, and she thanks the caribou for their generosity and never wastes any part of their bodies.

One year the couple moves far away from their village, and both become very busy with all that they have to do. The wife becomes so fatigued from all the work and the irksome mosquitoes that she cannot appreciate the summer. Exhausted, she begins to wish that her husband will not catch another caribou, for she is tired of drying the meat, storing it, and putting the skins on the racks. Just as she is thinking about her desperate condition, she sees an empty bucket that had been thrown away. Nearby is a caribou that her husband has just slain. On impulse, she puts the bucket over the caribou's head so that she won't have to deal with it further.

The next day, when her husband goes out to hunt, he has a difficult time finding a caribou. Inexplicably, the caribou seem to be very far away—so far away that the hunter comes home empty-handed. His former luck in hunting seems to desert him. Winter is approaching. With this unexpected bad luck, the hunter is afraid they may starve. Indeed, by the end of winter all of their food is gone. Since the couple has only sinew and skins left to chew on, they become weak. The hunter can hardly walk. Still, every day he goes off trying to find caribou.

To his surprise, one day he sees a strange apparition moving over the tundra. It is so dark that he can barely see. He thinks it might be another starving person, but as he approaches, he sees in amazement that it is a caribou with a bucket over its head. The caribou is making a lot of noise in its distress. Immediately, the hunter goes up to the animal and removes the bucket, whereupon the caribou tells the hunter that even though his wife has put the bucket over its head, the caribou will send him luck in hunting once again.

As promised, the next day the hunter finds a large caribou herd and takes one back to his camp. After his wife prepares it, she admits what she has done and says that she will never again do anything so foolish as to put a bucket over a caribou's head. The hunter's luck returns, and more caribou come to him. Meanwhile, the caribou that suffered from the bucket grazes nearby, even following the couple to their summer camp, although it seems to ignore them. Now that the hunter's wife has learned to be afraid of hunger and knows the importance of valuing and caring for the caribou, she always works hard, and the couple always has enough food. Eventually, the enigmatic caribou that showed them the importance of respect and gave them luck disappears one night and does not return.

This story emphasizes the importance of constant diligence, hard work, and the thankfulness and respectful care that are necessary in order to give back to the animals, in return for offering themselves to humans. Putting a bucket over the caribou's head shows disrespect for the animal and is an attempt to ignore or deny its presence. If we put ourselves in the caribou's place, we see that having a bucket put over our head is humiliating and shaming—an abusive way to treat others and to be treated ourselves.

Like the woman who puts the bucket over the caribou's head, we may neglect and insult an important part of our own psyches—our animal roots. Caring for our animal needs instead of ignoring them requires conscious attention. Instead of telling her husband that she is tired, the woman in this story just gives up. A bucket is a modern, man-made object that can be utilized to contain water, symbolic for tears and the flow of feelings. Instead, the bucket is misused to cover up the natural instincts, like crying, that want our attention.

The wife's exhaustion also shows the human need for respite from work. The wife's overworked condition is analogous to our own society's frenetic, fast-paced way of life, which is particularly exhausting to the feminine, receptive mode of being. Compulsive overwork that prevents us from enjoying the world around us is part of the spiritual dilemma from which we all suffer. The story shows how our own frustration can affect other people, as the wife's affected her husband's ability to hunt and could have led to physical and spiritual starvation. The wife's resentment has consequences beyond the material world, causing the supernatural caribou to suffer and withdraw the source of food. If such an attitude prevails on a wide scale, it affects the immediate community as well as the larger society of humankind—a difficult lesson that we are only beginning to learn in contemporary times.

This folk tale has relevance for our own society and our disdain for animal life. Companies that encroach on caribou migration routes in order to profit from the wealth of new oilfields abuse animal rights and threaten the caribou with extinction. Our frenetic race for material success, possessions, and technological advances has depleted the environment, harmed animals, and exhausted our own ability to connect to animal instincts. Just as, in the story, disregard for the caribou leaves the couple disconnected and without food, the neglected soul leaves us starving for meaning in our lives and thirsting for the spirit. The results of such insensitivity deaden spiritual consciousness.

How wonderful that the hunter finally is able to notice the suffering animal and lift the bucket from its head! Today many of us have lost faith that we can repair what has been neglected. But this story shows that even something so mysterious as the extraordinary caribou that come and go according to their own nature will allow us to care for them and thereby revive our lost souls.

A contemporary Caribou Eskimo man expresses the importance of relating to the animals and laments modern society's lack of understanding them: "Now-days, look around. Animals are insulted. They might go away forever. This can happen. It is not like when I was a child. People don't understand animals anymore. People who have to go among animals, out on the land, they still understand. Animals are people like us. They can die out. And not come back."[6]

The challenge of hunting faced by Arctic people is to accept the risk of an arduous expedition that might entail death. Hunting is a journey from which the hunter might not return. To be successful, the hunter needs to be alert, courageous, vigilant, skillful, intuitive, and patient. This means that the hunter must learn the art of waiting until the animal is ready to come and offer itself to him.

Yielding to Nature, rather than confronting or controlling it, is a major part of the art of hunting. Moving with the environment, not mastering it, is the essential moral and spiritual attitude that honors the ancient agreement with the animals who offer themselves to the hunter. Greed—that is, taking more than one needs—insulting animals, or behaving badly toward them or the earth by not allowing it to rest so the land can restore itself for the animals—all are violations of the sacred trust and reciprocity between animals and humans. Observing taboos, offering songs and poems of praise to honor and thank the animals in gratitude, and ritual preparation of the slain creature so its spirit can return to the earth are all part of the sacred pact between hunter and hunted.[7]

The Japanese film *Dersu Uzala,* directed by Akira Kurosawa, shows the life of a Siberian Goldi hunter and the wisdom and friendship he gives to a Russian cartographer through the model of his life in the forest. Dersu approaches a group of Russians in the dense taiga while they are trying to map out some routes. The captain of the Russian crew realizes that the Goldi hunter, an old man, can help them in their project since he knows the ways of the wilderness. When the captain asks the hunter to guide them, Dersu accepts and starts off through the forest. He sees tracks of animals that the Russians do not observe; he can tell who has passed by before them, even the age of the person; and he teaches the captain how to notice these important details necessary to their task and to survival.

When they come upon a shelter in the forest and use some wood inside to build a fire and warm themselves, Dersu reminds them to gather more wood and to leave matches and rice for the next person who may need refuge; he emphasizes the importance of giving help to strangers. After eating, when one of the Russians starts to throw the crumbs into the fire, Dersu rushes to salvage the food; he tells the Russians that the birds or the squirrels might want it.

When they find an abandoned trap with dead animals in it, Dersu shakes his head in sorrow, saying that it is wrong to kill animals for no purpose. Finding the tracks of a tiger, Dersu honors the beast and asks the tiger to stay away. He doesn't want to have to kill this magnificent animal. For Dersu, the whole universe is alive, including the smallest grain of earth. He honors the sun and the moon because he knows that if they die, so will everything else. While on their journey, Dersu saves the captain's life. When the captain tries to thank him specially, Dersu replies that they are all struggling for survival together. Doing the things one must do to survive in the forest is a natural part of life, not something to boast about.

After the land has been mapped out, the Russian cartographers return to the city, thank Dersu, and part with him at the edge of the forest. Time passes, but the captain holds the image of Dersu and his wisdom in his heart. Years later, the captain is sent on another mapping mission in the forest. He has the good fortune to encounter the Goldi hunter again. Much older now, Dersu comes upon the Russians while hunting, and the captain asks the Goldi hunter to help them a second time. Now the captain has a chance to help Dersu, as the aging hunter had helped him.

Dersu's eyes begin to fail him, and several times while hunting he misses hitting his prey. At first the old hunter can't believe it. In despair he asks: "How will I live in the forest?" Soon afterward, he notices that a tiger is nearby, and he realizes they are in danger. Once more he entreats the tiger to stay away, but the huge carnivorous cat looms before his eyes, and the threatened Dersu takes a shot. In dread, convinced that he has wounded or even killed the beast, Dersu asks the forest spirit, whom the Goldi worship, for forgiveness for injuring the great Usuri tiger whose presence graces the Siberian forest.

Haunted by this unnecessary shooting, along with the realization that he is getting old and that his failing capacities now make him a liability in the forest, Dersu becomes morose. To assuage Dersu's despair, the captain invites his forest friend and mentor to be a part of his family and to come and live in his city home. Not knowing what else to do, the aging Dersu accepts the offer. At first Dersu is happy to be with the captain and his family, and he takes pleasure in teaching the captain's son all that he knows about the wilds. But he misses the forest. When he pitches a tent so that he can sleep outside in nature, he is told that the city laws forbid it. Nor is he allowed to shoot his gun to practice in order to see if he can regain his skill. Once more, the Goldi becomes depressed.

In desperation, Dersu tells his cherished friends that he must leave. "I don't like to live in a box; there is no air to breathe," he tries to explain to the captain and his family, who have come to realize that the city will never be a home for Dersu. In sorrow, the family waves farewell as the old man leaves for the nearby woods that surround the city. The captain comprehends that their beloved Goldi hunter may be returning to the forest to die in his wilderness home.

At the film's end, the captain is informed that Dersu is dead. He goes to the woods at the edge of the city, where the hunter's body has been found. There he discovers that the modern gun that he had given to Dersu has been stolen. The captain gave Dersu the new gun so that the old man would be able to see and take aim better, enabling him to hunt well and protect himself in the forest. At the site, the official in charge of the burial waits impatiently for the captain to finish burying the dead man. Alone, the captain suspects that Dersu most probably was shot by a greedy person who stole the new gun from the old hunter. The captain buries Dersu in grief—an anguish shared by all those viewers who recognize the irreplaceable spirit of the Siberian forest man.

Dersu Uzala, like the Reindeer People, embodies the part of ourselves that knows how to be at home and survive in Nature—an interior organic wisdom with which many of us seem to have lost touch. The city officials, impatient with the old indigenous hunter, represent the tendencies of modern civilization to encroach upon the natural environment and its inhabitants through artificial rules and limits that violate the ways of Nature.

The killer of Dersu Uzala personifies the greed of modern man, who will even destroy life for material gain. Our hope lies with the captain and his Russian team, who grow to love Dersu as they recognize and value the Goldi's sagacity and who know their lives depend on it. The captain represents our human capacity to honor and preserve instinctive intelligence, courage, and compassion—wisdom essential to our survival and necessary to transform the greed that may destroy our civilization.

The Arctic offers us the gift of adversity, so that we may develop and sometimes even surpass the borders of our potential. The Far North is a direction of the soul that calls upon all of our resources to survive. It requires us to be conscious, courageous, and compassionate. Survival in this exacting environment necessitates resilience and persistence, providing opportunities to become strong and resourceful, and to struggle through our own effort. Yet it also enjoins us to cooperate, obliging us to work together as a community to survive. It compels us to make choices for which we alone are responsible, while knowing that those choices affect others. In the extreme, it summons us to change. The Far North demands our trust and humility in the face of Nature's ineffable ways, as well as trust in our own mysterious human nature.

Twelve

TIME AND HOME
ON THE TUNDRA

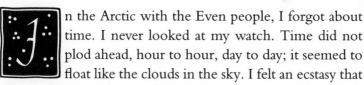I n the Arctic with the Even people, I forgot about time. I never looked at my watch. Time did not plod ahead, hour to hour, day to day; it seemed to float like the clouds in the sky. I felt an ecstasy that I had never experienced before. Since it was summer, light was ever present, changing with the shimmering reflections of the sun on the mountains of stone. It was as though everything stood out from time in the true sense of the word *ecstasy—ec-stasis,* "to stand out beyond particular beings." Being there was like being in an altered state; yet I had taken no drug to induce this effect. I was filled with wonder. The reindeer, their people, and their land—life itself—was offering me its greatest gift.

Time in reindeer country is a quite different phenomenon from technological clock time. For the people of the Arctic, time is neither measured by linear standards nor calculated in the mechanical manner of clock time. Instead, the Arctic people perceive time as cyclical, reflecting the way Nature manifests the passage of the seasons. I learned this lesson on my trip to Lapland. In autumn the Sami round up the reindeer and mark the newborn calves. I asked a reindeer herdress exactly when and where the reindeer roundup would take place because I wanted to experience it. She laughed and said: "We have a different sense of time that follows the reindeer's rhythms. We never know exactly which day it will happen. But we can feel it in the air on the morning when the reindeer are ready. On that day, we have the roundup."

Because reindeer and caribou are sacred to the people of the Far North, some groups distinguish the months according to the journey and the development of these beloved animals. In Canada, the Barren Ground Inuit mark the beginning of their calendar year with the arrival of the caribou herds early in May.[1] Early May, the first of sixteen stages in their year, is the time of the "moon in which the caribou go down" from the forests.

The Barren Ground Inuit call the second month (June) the "divided moon," since this is a transitional time when some of the ground is covered with snow while other land is bare, and when some waters are still frozen while others have thawed. In early July, their third month, new hair starts to show beneath the old hair in the caribou's fur. This is the time of "caribou skins with two kinds of hair."

The fourth month, "the one with the open mouth," occurs around late July, when the Inuit see baby birds with open beaks, waiting in their nests for their mothers to feed them. "The moon in which the caribou come," in August, is the fifth month; it begins when new caribou herds arrive from the lakes and plains nearby.

Toward the end of August and early September, Inuit hunters are alert to the sixth month, which they call "the moon in which the caribou have a medium coat." Antler velvet marks the seventh month, around late September, when the velvet starts to shed from the antlers—"the moon in which the caribou antlers lose their skin."

Then comes "the moon in which it begins to be cool," when ice forms on small bodies of water in early October (the eighth month). Late October, the ninth month, is marked by "the moon in which the big lakes begin to cover over," the time when larger lakes and rivers start to freeze.

The exciting tenth month (November) is "the moon in which the caribou mate." Around December, when bulls start to shed their antlers, the eleventh month is called "the moon in which the antlers fall from the caribou bulls."

The end of January and early February, the time when fetuses are developing in the pregnant caribou, demarcate the twelfth month, which is called "the moon in which something is laid in."

When the coldest temperatures occur in late February and early March, the thirteenth month is called "abortion moon." In this frigid period the pregnant caribou can miscarry. The next month of "the nameless moon" distinguishes the dangerous time when humans are most likely to suffer from starvation. During this fourteenth month, the importance of following spiritual teaching is emphasized.

April is the fifteenth month—the time when the caribou begin their annual migration northward—and is called "the moon in which the caribou must begin to go through the country." The last month occurs in early May, "the moon in which the roofs fall down." This is the time when the sun is warm and strong enough to melt the ice and snow houses of the Inuit.

The sixteenth month passes once more into the first month of the Inuit calendar, when the caribou begin their yearly journey anew. Thus, for the Inuit people, time flows naturally with the caribou's annual trek across the tundra to give birth.

Far away, across the Bering strait in Lapland, the Sami people identify eight seasons, distinguished in part by the weather and the sun's cycle, which the reindeer follow instinctively on their journey to give birth.

In spring-winter (around April), when the ice begins to melt, the reindeer start out on their journey. By midspring, the pregnant reindeer are streaming across the Arctic tundra on their way to the calving grounds. They begin to give birth in spring-summer, late May and early June, when they reach the mountains.

During midsummer the reindeer and their young are busy gorging on grass and berries in the mountain pastures, constantly on the move in order to escape from the pestering black flies and mosquitoes. In autumn-summer, as the sun begins its descent in the heavens, the reindeer start to return to the lower lands.

Autumn is the time when the Sami mark the calves and take meat, before the bulls' hormones increase for the rutting season, making the meat unpalatable. Autumn-winter is the marginal time of safe weather, before the freezing time approaches. Then, in midwinter, the reindeer must struggle to survive, digging through ice and snow with their hooves for the lichen that sustains them until they are able to begin their birthing journey anew.

Experiencing time according to the rhythms of nature, as the reindeer people do, can put us back in touch with the intrinsic tempos of bodily and spiritual life and the cadence of the cosmos. In the course of my own spiritual and creative life, I have learned that I must honor the innate needs and pace of my body and soul, and the way that whatever book I am writing wants to take.

Sometimes growth is like the "moon in which the caribou mate"—creative energies are really moving; I feel the time of wedding in my soul. Often I feel a new birth is coming, as in the time of "the moon in which something is laid in." Other times are like the "abortion moon" period—frigid times when spiritual and creative life is in danger of miscarrying. At those times I feel I am in the "month of the nameless moon," the dangerous time when starvation seems imminent and I am plunged into the Dark Night of the Soul. Yet I know that if I am patient and endure this time of emptiness by being alert, I will receive renewal and more clarity.

Doing my work of spiritual honing in the "moon in which the caribou antlers lose their skin" will prepare me for the new growth that can come out of the Dark Night and will fortify me for the time when "the caribou begin their journey to give birth." When I am able to experience and perceive time with such images of Nature, I am able to surrender my ego-oriented linear wish to control exactly when and how things should happen. By letting go, I can open my eyes, arms, and heart to receive and be embraced by those forces of creation that never cease to surprise me and that are greater than anything I can plan or command.

While I was with the reindeer people, I also gained wisdom about the meaning of home. They experience home in a unique way: Home is wherever the reindeer are. For example, the Sami people build their traditional summer dwellings, which they call *ghoati,* from birch branches, which they cover with earthen sod or reindeer hides. They layer their floor with birch twigs, and they sleep on reindeer skins. The *ghoati* is a round enclosure, adapted to the environment, that does not disturb the land. The Sami people dismantle it when they need to move on.

As we traveled through Lapland, we saw many teepee-shaped structures made from bare birch branches that were left open to the air. These were "homes" in which Sami families had stayed, then moved on, and to which they might return on their next annual journey. As one Sami reported, "These things aren't built to last, and that's the Sami view of the world. We leave no traces to show where we have been. Home is in the mountain pastures in summer and the coastal forests in winter, wherever the reindeer are. Home is not a dwelling, but a sense of the land that I recognize as a part of me."[2]

The nomadic reindeer people of the Siberian tundra have portable homes that they call *chooms.* A *choom* is a cone-shaped tent made of reindeer skins placed across an earthen floor, on a frame of about thirty or more sticks or bones. It measures four to six yards in diameter. Near the sea, the *choom* is called a *yaranga,* and the maritime people living there construct it out of walrus hides. The Yakut people call their houses *yurtas,* which are low huts made of mud or clay, while the Eskimo people build their domelike homes, called *igloos,* from blocks of frozen snow.[3]

When we met the Even people in the wilderness, they were camped in a mountain pasture, following the reindeer on their way south. But even though they would disband this temporary camp in a few days to move on, they felt at home there. "Look here," said the elder, pointing to the reindeer as they came running toward us. "Here is our home among the reindeer. Welcome!" We felt at home, too, during the time we were there. Truly I felt more comfortable and relaxed, more at peace, in this remote wilderness, sitting and sleeping on the earth, surrounded by these mystical antlered creatures and the people who cherished them ardently, than I had in my childhood abode and in most of the city dwellings I had inhabited.

Home—what is it? Where is it, really? I began to wonder. For some time, I had been searching for a place where I might settle permanently. I had been besieged with dreams of homes collapsing, of homes that were not comfortable or that had been broken into, of homes so dangerous that I could not invite my friends to stay, and of homes where I could not find pasture for my horses. Home was an enigma to me, especially since I had grown up in a household that was emotionally unpredictable and even dangerous. As an adult, I had lived in many locations in the United States as well as in other countries.

The places where I felt most at home, wherever I was, tended to be outdoors in nature. I felt most at home while I was hiking, cross-country skiing, or riding my horse. Some-times, however, I would feel at home in a beautiful city like Paris, wandering along the river or through intriguing alleys that might open suddenly to reveal a lovely fountain or the brilliant stained-glass windows of a cathedral. Home, too, might be in a concert hall, listening to a transporting con-certo, or in a room where I could read or delight in a work of art. Home was in dialogue with my friends, and especially with my companion, Keith. Yet I had also found home in cafés where I wrote, and even unexpectedly in the Paris Metro, where I felt connected with other people by the human bond that unites us all.

Home, I realized, while I was sitting with the smiling Evens, who spoke a different language, and while surrounded by my antlered animal friends, is where my heart opens up. Home is where I can stretch out to others, as the antlers of the reindeer branch out to the heavens. Or it is where I reach inward to the depths of my soul, so that I can traverse beyond my limited viewpoint and commence the great inner and outer journey, like the one that the reindeer undertake every year to give birth.

To be at home is to move and grow as life requires it, to change with the demands of inner psychic development, with the outer needs of community, and with the earth on which we dwell. To be at home is to live attentively, to listen to the beating heart of the mythical reindeer doe, hidden in the center of the earth. It is to live near the gentle heart that knows how to bear suffering, yet how to love and radiate with rapture as well.

Do we Westerners, too, have in our psyches a time and a place that is nomadic, that corresponds to the way in which the reindeer people move, centered both practically and spiritually on the animals that they follow? Nomadic time focuses upon survival and is centered upon "something that moves." It follows the rhythms of nature. Home would be where we can feel "creation's heartbeat" and listen to its melodies.

Traveling in the Arctic and living with the Even people gave me a feeling of what it might mean to live in this way. It suggested that the Far North is really a direction of the soul. In conversations with many men and women from different areas of the world, I discovered that people frequently dream of the Far North as a place of vision, as a locale that challenges the questing spirit and offers a unique understanding of our human purpose, tasks, and calling. Many feel summoned to the North as an essential part of a search for meaning. There the paradoxes of existence are revealed in all their extremity. Remembering the creation story of the reindeer doe, I wondered: "In the map of the human heart, does the compass point north?"

Thirteen

ARCTIC VISION

hile I was in the Arctic with the reindeer peoples, a sense of spiritual peace flowed into me. The reindeer, resplendent in their antlered crowns, overwhelmed me with their beauty. The generosity of the Even touched me deeply. They shared their way of life freely, despite their arduous lives on the edge of survival in the wildlands. Their humble strength, their kindness, and their simplicity awed me. How could they live so serenely, I wondered, in the face of the terrors of the Arctic—the vast isolation, the constant threat of erratic weather, the extremes of temperature, and the ceaseless search for food? Yet being there, I sensed that the Arctic is a hidden paradise.

Looking around, I could see the tundra as a "secret garden." It reminded me of the children's book in which some emotionally abandoned children find a secret garden that gives them beauty, solace, and hope and that enriches their lives and imagination and enables their survival, despite the bleakness in their ordinary lives.

Here in the Far North, where I was now, I saw that this Arctic garden, unknown and unexplored by so many people, was splashed with subtle color. The earth glistened with gray rock, covered with yellow and lavender lichen. Golden-green moss pillows and brownish orange bushes burning with rust-red berries decorated the land. The rocky riverbeds were strewn with rounded shiny stones, as though a phantom gardener had arranged them in special places, part of a grand design for this celestial landscape. Crystal-clear green water ran in rivulets around these stone sculptures, revealing underground springs, blessed fountains that adorn the Far North's summer spectacle.

The reindeer are the flowers of the tundra. Their streaming antlers look like ancient plant roots turned upside down, swaying in the sky, or tree branches flying through the heavens. The clattering of their antlers sounds like the beating of a shaman's rattle. Seen from a distance, the reindeer running on the misty mountains seem like spirits that appear, then vanish back into the ether. The clouds shift shape in the northern sky, showing ever-changing faces of the ethereal specter. The northern lights prompt the heavens to shimmer.

Gathered around the campfire with the Even people, sitting on reindeer skins and sharing food and stories with them, watching them work together cheerfully and tend the reindeer with love, we all were thankful for the splendor of this polar Garden of Eden. As Keith and I looked at the moving canopy of antlers, then at the swaying branches of the trees above us, we understood that the reindeer are the center of the Even's world, the spiritual adornment of the world tree around which their universe revolves. When a bird flew near, alighting on a branch to sing, it was a melodious message in which we all reveled. Together we delighted in the aroma of Mother Arctic's secret garden. Every breeze brought an exotic fragrance; every gust of wild wind reminded us of our relative safety, our finitude, and our impermanence in this polar paradise.

As we sat together in the midst of the tundra, entranced by its wild spaces and primeval secrets, I began to comprehend what it can mean for a person's life to be enfolded in the arms of Nature, to be a part of an ineffable mystery, so great and so beautiful that it is terrifying. Here, at the edge of the world near the North Pole, I suddenly remembered a startling dream that had come to me a decade earlier, in another hemisphere in the tropics.

I was at the volcano park on the island of Hawaii, and I dreamed that I *saw* the face of divinity. The dream came to me before daybreak, when I wanted to awaken to see the sunrise over the rim of the volcano before hiking down its crater. In the dream, thinking I was awake, I rushed to the window to see the sunrise. To my surprise, a great glacier formed on the side of the volcano. The colors radiated supernatural energy: purple, violet, electric blue, orange, magenta, red, fuchsia, pink, gold, white. Suddenly I knew that I was looking directly at the face of the divine. But its brilliance was too great for me to bear. My body was thrown backward a hundred yards by a mighty force. The jolt shocked me like a lightning bolt. I could look no longer, only try to save my life, and I crawled on hands and knees in dread back to my bed. As I awakened, still shaking, I realized that I had been allowed a moment's vision of the ineffable—a sublime and terrible moment that was more than my finite self could endure.

The dream brought back the opening lines of Rilke's elegiac *Duino Elegies*.

W HO, if I cried, would hear me among the angelic
orders? And even if one of them suddenly
pressed me against his heart, I should fade in the strength of his
stronger existence. For Beauty's nothing
but beginning of Terror we're still just able to bear,
and why we adore it so is because it serenely
disdains to destroy us. Each single angel is terrible.
And so I keep down my heart, and swallow the call-note
of depth-dark sobbing. Alas, who is there
we can make use of? Not angels, not men;
and already the knowing brutes are aware
that we don't feel very securely at home
within our interpreted world.[1]

Rilke's expression of fear and trembling before the inscrutable paradox of beauty and terror speaks to my dream of the transcendent glacier-volcano that contained the incomprehensible—the numinous opposites of volcanic fire and glacial ice, an image so powerful that it stunned me.

The poem also touched my experience in the Siberian wilderness. The difference I experienced there, after following the antlered ones, was that the Arctic's angelic messengers, the reindeer, *are* accessible. And our human counterparts, the reindeer people, are able to feel and to affirm the soul's "I–Thou" relationship with these antlered angels. In the midst of one of the most forbidding, treacherous, isolated, and vast stretches of wilderness on earth, the reindeer people are able to live in harmony, ever in touch with impending death, yet all the while celebrating life. Just as the couple in "The Woman Who Put the Bucket Over the Caribou's Head" learned to thank and esteem the enigmatic caribou that held the mystery of the source of food and of life, so the Arctic people respect the transcendent nature of these animal angels, praising them along with all of the gifts of earthly existence.

The Duino Elegies lament the dreadful alienation of humankind in one of the most powerful elegiac expressions of human vulnerability in Western literature. Rilke needed ten years to record this poetic cycle, which enabled him to affirm *all* of existence. He learned that the task of wandering humans—a challenge that the nomadic reindeer people already know and accept—is to celebrate the simple things of the earth and to transform fleeting beings and experiences by acknowledging permanence in spirit. By praising their existence through the sacred word, holy image, or reverential ritual, we can change them within our hearts. In this way we can make them part of ourselves as we, in turn, become part of the whole. This is the Earth's urgent command: Transform! This spiritual venture is the *adventure* that is at once the call and the gift of the reindeer and its people.

The adventure of the wilderness gives us the certainty that we are guests on this earth. If you hike into wilderness areas in the Rocky Mountains, at the beginning of the trail you will see a sign that describes the parameters of humans vis-à-vis the wilderness. The statement from the National Wilderness Act emphasizes that humans who enter the wilderness are indeed only Nature's privileged guests, who must respect their responsibility in passing into these wild lands. The fact that we must have such signs in our country points to the alienation of Western civilization from Nature, for it indicates that some who previously set foot in the sacred wilds abused nature by either strewing trash or taking away its precious plants, trees, or animals. Many who dared to enter the wild lands unaware of Nature's mightiness and dangers, or unprepared for extreme changes in weather and terrain, have been severely injured or died. Those who have camped out or trekked in the wilderness for any length of time experience how vulnerable they are before the greater powers of Nature.

Being in the wilderness reminds us that we are not the midpoint of the Great Chain of Being, not even the main point, but only part of the whole. Human lives are frail before glaring sun, blasting wind, lightning bolt, freezing storm, blinding snow, glacial avalanche, river torrent, relentless sea, darkening night, haunting moon.

Surviving in the cyclical processes of Nature entails holding life and death together, as Arctic peoples do. When the Even place the bodies of their dead in the leafy arms of a tree, to be guided by the reindeer spirit to the celestial realm, they acknowledge, through ritual, the great round of life and death—the paradox of existence in which they participate every day. From the reindeer people I received the gift of knowing that life renews itself if you stay within the cycle. In order to survive, the Even people must stay within the flow of natural events and be attentive every moment. Their dedicated focus on something greater than their own immediate gratification—the reindeer that they love, care for, and follow—organizes their lives individually and communally and gives them purpose and meaning.

The reindeer are the living transcendent reality around

which their lives revolve. By living their myths, which center on the reindeer, they are guided by the gentle spirit embodied by this animal. Listening to the reindeer doe's heartbeat, as in the Sami creation myth, elicits in them compassion and gratitude for one another, for the plants and animals, for the earth, and for all life. Following the reindeer directs the members of the community to a life of conscious cooperation. Alert, attentive care for the reindeer and for the earth upon which they run is the constant guide for their awareness. Among the Even people, I saw joy in their eyes as they tended to the reindeer. To care for something greater than ourselves—the reindeer—is the gift. To be centered not on personal ego concerns but on the good of the reindeer, the community, and the earth takes us beyond our limited viewpoints.

Spiritual life is a journey, just like the reindeer's yearly run to the mountains. On our human travels we sometimes lose our sense of direction, become distracted, or forget our purpose. Times like these can be as terrifying as discovering we are lost in the wilderness. The spiritual journey *is* like a wilderness trek, just as the psyche is like the wildlands. But as Jung once said, the psyche does have a sense of direction. If we attend to the psyche with care by listening to the messages that come from dreams and life experiences, we can learn to survive its savage nights. The reindeer that knows its way to the birthing grounds can serve as a spirit guide that gives direction and meaning to a much larger reality and can be a solace in these lost, tormented times. Through imagination, we can open up to our earthly adventure by following the reindeer.

Life on earth is a mystery. We all quest for, search for the meaning of why we are here. In the end we are all nomads, traveling the wildlands of our existence, exploring the outer limits, trying to find the center. With birth at one end and death at the other, we wander about, trying to make sense of our lives. If we can accept the wanderer in us, we will learn to love the holy fool whose wisdom is so valued and appreciated in Russia and in India. Venturing into the psyche's vast spaces and daring to explore the world around us, we can enter into a spiritual freedom and maturity that is as vast and boundless as the tundra. Wandering, we finally will discern, is really wondering at the glories of existence.

For this venture, the reindeer can serve as an imaginal guide, for they are symbolic of the soul's journey, uniting spiritual life and Nature. Biologically considered in its instinctive destiny as birth-giving journeyer, and shamanically viewed as messenger between the earth and heavens and as bearer of the dead to the spirit world, the reindeer continually cycles between the poles of life and death. Just as reindeer must move over treacherous terrain before they reach the welcoming mountain meadows where their babies are born every spring, so our soul's passage requires that we negotiate the rapids of despair. We must learn to move between the extremities of possibility and necessity, spirit and matter, and infinitude and finitude, as Kierkegaard would express it.

I found myself plunged anew into this paradox of spirit and matter while I was in the midst of writing this book, when my mother died. I was the last of her family line, and my sense of security was shaken. An old apprehension of poverty resurfaced with intensity. Had my mother's stable existence protected me all these years? Would I lose all the professional and economic security for which I had worked so hard? I had dedicated my time and energy to writing books to share with others whatever I had learned through my struggles. Now I felt raw and vulnerable. I doubted whether I had any vision to offer. Could I write another book? Could I even finish this one?

The darkening of my own soul revolved around the despair resulting from my mother's death. But it also extended to the World's Dark Night, to our ecological crisis, to the wounds of Gaia, the cosmic mother, and to the reindeer's plight. My despondency about my mother's death and about the possible extinction of the reindeer seemed connected through their mutual basic nature, the maternal instinct. The reindeer's innate maternal drive to journey so far for the sake of giving life—an inborn effort that takes them across hundreds of miles—reminded me of my mother's tenacity for survival—for herself and for that of her family whom she supported for years by working at minimum wages.

The loss of my mother and my despondency over the threat to the reindeer species and the reindeer people finally coalesced in an urgent question: Why is that which gives so abundantly—the generous spirit—that which is so abused? When we see life doing whatever it can to give birth— whether it is the reindeer, the maternal capacity in our human selves, or ultimately the earth, our common mother—why do we contaminate it? Why do the earth and her tender reindeer have to suffer from humans' ecological abuse? Is the reindeer doe's heart, buried deep in the earth according to the Sami creation myth, now beating with pain and grief? How ironic, I began to think, that the endangered reindeer were the earthly embodiment of the spiritual journey between the visible finite world and the invisible infinite realm, whose existence I had begun to doubt.

After my mother's death I had to relearn how to hold

together the tension between life and death as a whole, and to renew my belief in the spirit-world. My mother was no longer visible. "Where is she?" I asked, as I cried myself to sleep every night. Was it still true, as Rilke claimed, that one of our prime spiritual tasks on earth is to bridge the visible and invisible realms? Do we really stand on the threshold between the transitory and the eternal, between heaven and earth? Could death truly be the "holiest inspiration," as the poet had said?

Several years earlier, when I was in Lapland, I had been told that my mother had to undergo serious surgery. While driving on an isolated road along the edge of a Finnish forest, I was worrying about her impending operation. Keith and I were looking for a room to stay for the night and, even harder to find, a phone so that I could make a call to the United States to talk to her. Just then, amid these concerns, we realized that we had no idea where we actually were. It was dusk, and we were anxious and lost in a forest of dwarfed trees—just at that time when unexpected things occur. Instead of the alarming things that we feared, however, a brilliant sunset began to brighten a mountain to our left with purple, gold, and rust hues. We stopped the car to get our bearings. Turning around, we saw a magnificent white reindeer standing in the road behind us, its antlers illumined by the golden sunset. At that moment, I felt a mystical bond between the reindeer and my mother. Then Keith sighed: "Your mother will come through this time." Encountering the white reindeer, a living symbol of the soul's life after death, assuaged my worries about her surgery. The synchronicity of seeing it shortly before her operation felt like a good omen. The white reindeer seemed like a guardian angel. My mother came through the operation fine.

Now, as I remembered the white reindeer—its link with my mother and its sign of hope for me—my consciousness began to shift. I thought of the film *Pathfinder,* one of the few foreign films I had ever seen with my mother. We had seen it together in Philadelphia, a year or so after her operation. In the film, the white reindeer appears to the shaman in a vision three times: once as a youth, once in midlife, and once before his death. Then it reappears to the young hero who takes the older shaman's place. Had the white reindeer shown itself to me in Lapland not only as a sign of hope that my mother would live through that particular operation, but also as a message of her impending passage to the other world? Had the white reindeer come to call upon me to affirm the meaning of her final journey from the earth? Had it appeared as a sign of promise that I could evoke later, to help me to continue my own spiritual journey on earth? Ancient Sami lore holds the white reindeer to be the soul of a dead person returned to life. In Buddhist belief, those who have reached enlightenment, the bodhisattvas, return to earth to help others to attain this level of spiritual awareness. Was the white reindeer like a bodhisattva, returning to earth to remind us of the secret of compassion? Was this one of the reindeer's precious gifts to me, a doubting earthling?

Recalling this experience, I also remembered some words of Rilke in *Letters to a Young Poet.*[2]

We must assume our existence as *broadly* as we in any way can: everything, even the unheard-of must be possible in it. That is at bottom the only courage that is demanded of us: to have courage for the most strange, the most singular and the most inexplicable that we may encounter. That mankind has in this sense been cow-

ardly has done life endless harm; the experiences that
are called "visions," the whole so-called "spirit-world,"
death, all those things that are so closely akin to us, have
by daily parrying been so crowded out of life that the
senses with which we could have grasped them are
atrophied. But fear of the inexplicable has not alone
impoverished the existence of the individual; the relation between one human being and another has also
been cramped by it; only someone who is ready for
everything, who excludes nothing, not even the most
enigmatical, will live the relation to another as something alive and will himself draw exhaustively from his
own existence.

The white reindeer, my mother's death, Keith's dream of
the reindeer woman and the outer journey that this dream
initiated, my own dream in which hundreds of reindeer came
running to me, the unparalleled gift of finding the reindeer
people in Siberia on their way through the vast Arctic wilderness, the call to write about all this in order to make sense
of it—all were inexplicable offerings from a greater source.
To be ready for such offerings, even for the most enigmatic
conundrum—the link between life and death—is the challenge of being human.

The readiness to be open, to be here, to be alive, to embark on the birthing journey is just as essential to "I–Thou"
relationships of the soul as it is to the quest to follow the
reindeer. I understood now that this was the core of the
spiritual journey initiated by the dream of the reindeer. The
reindeer had come through dream life to invite me to follow
them, to attract me to their strange, unfathomable way
through the wilderness: to journey without reservation, to

plunge like the mystics into the abyss and climb out, and finally to take the leap of faith over the chasm of despair to the shore of hope; to open to both ecstasy and travail, to bear witness to the bloody antlers announcing birth, death, and renewal, to hear the mythic reindeer doe's heart beating in the center of the earth, and to open to love.

Thus pondering about the reindeer, I reflected on the fundamental gift my mother had given me—the gift of life and the possibility to love. Just as the reindeer's purpose is to journey to give birth, so my mother was my birth-giver. The passage through her womb was my opening into life. Just as I was confronted now with the closure of her earthly body, so my life's journey entailed facing the ultimate frontier—death. The privilege of living, of being fully alive in the moment, alert to the other side, death, brought with it a sense of vital presence and possibility, which my mother bequeathed to me fifty-odd years ago and which the reindeer and their people far away in the wilderness once again showed me.

On the day that we left the Even people and the reindeer, the Siberian elder gave us a parting gift. Knowing that Keith was a doctor, the elder had asked him a favor. The elder was concerned about the physical condition of his heart because he had suffered a heart attack several years earlier; now he was in the wilderness, far away from medical facilities, and he was worried about some recurring symptoms. Keith offered to listen to his heart. He put his ear to the elder's chest, tapped his back, touched the old man's wrist gently to feel his pulse, and found his heart to be in good condition. The elder was grateful for his help. In thanks he gave us a necklace of bear gallstones, along with a vial of bear blood and a paw. "Bear are sacred," the elder told us. "Wear this necklace, which circles the heart, to remember us and to protect the heart and its health."

Caring, the heart's task—this is the pivotal gift that I received from following the reindeer, meeting their people, and continuing on this spiritual trek. My heart has opened to a new dimension in the course of this soul's journey. Whenever I lose my balance, the reindeer image offers me solace and healing. Then I feel stronger, more grounded, centered in a new way. I can sense life's primal energy as it surges from the reindeer doe's heartbeat deep in the earth, courses through my body, and continues through my new spiritual antlers, to open me up to the mysteries of that which is most familiar on earth and that which is strange and wondrous. The reindeer call me to run with them on their journey to give birth and to roam wherever the spirit summons me.

Now, long after returning from the Arctic wilderness, I can receive the gift of this journey with all my heart. For I can still see deep into the tender wild eyes of the reindeer and feel the love of the Even people, who cherish these beautiful animals and the earth upon which they run. I know that I have been given the miracle of glimpsing and experiencing a timeless moment of paradise in this Siberian Shangri-la. And a dream that I had while camping in the wilderness with the Even and the reindeer seems to bear witness to this expansion of my heart.

I dreamed that an ancient Asian master of Tai Chi was dancing on the mountain and invited me to join him. He put his arms around me, and we danced ecstatically in a circle. I felt his love, but then I began to doubt that this could happen to me, and I questioned whether he truly loved me. He answered my doubt by looking straight into my eyes and kissing me deeply as we continued to dance in the wilderness endlessly. At dawn, I awoke and looked out of my tent into the soft deep eyes of the reindeer grazing nearby.

Now whenever I am plunged into hopelessness and despair, I try to bring these images of hope and beauty to consciousness. I can remember dancing over the mountain with the Tai Chi master. I can see the beautiful eyes of the reindeer running wild over the tundra with their swaying antlered crowns. I can hear the reindeer mothers calling to their calves, and I can smell the fresh Arctic air and the perfume of the berries, bushes, and grass. And I can hear the kind voice and see the loving eyes and gestures of the Even elder and of all the reindeer people as they invite us to join to celebrate spring's rebirth along with all of Nature's cycles. Together we are all prancing in a joyful jig on the mossy floor of the tundra's grand ballroom in that great eternal round—the reindeer dance.

Notes

Chapter 2 SPIRIT GUIDE

1. Fyodor Dostoyevsky, *The Brothers Karamazov,* trans. Constance Garnett (New York: Random House, 1950), p. 383.

2. Frank Waters, *The Man Who Killed the Deer* (Athens, OH: Swallow Press/Ohio University Press, 1970), p. 24.

Chapter 3 CREATION'S HEARTBEAT

1. W. H. Auden, "The Fall of Rome," in *Collected Poems,* Edward Mendelson, ed. (New York: Random House, 1947).

2. Johan Turi and Per Turi, *Lappish Texts,* ed. Emílie Demant-Hatt (Copenhagen: Host and Son, 1920).

3. The name for Beijen-neite is spelled differently in different sections of Lapland. For example, in the articles cited in the above referenced book, the spelling is Biejin-niedje. I have consistently used the spelling, Beijen-neite, since it appears first in this tale cited in footnote 4 that way, in order to avoid confusion.

4. See *Lapland Legends: Tales of an Ancient Race and Its Great Gods,* retold from the Swedish by Leonne de Cambrey. A rendering from the Solsönernas Saga of Valdemar Lindholm (Göteborg, 1909).

5. For a detailed discussion of the World's Dark Night and the Dark Night of the Soul, see my *Witness to the Fire: Creativity and the Veil of Addiction* (Boston: Shambhala Publications, 1989).

6. Quoted in Evelyn Underhill, *Mysticism* (New York: New American Library, 1974), p. 340.

7. Rainer Maria Rilke, *Letters to a Young Poet,* trans. M. D. Herter Norton (New York: W. W. Norton, 1963), pp. 53–54.

Chapter 4 MESSENGERS OF TRANSFORMATION

1. See John Berger's analysis in "Why Look at Animals?" in *About Looking* (New York: Vintage Books, 1980), pp. 3–28.

2. Louis Charbonneau-Lassay, *The Bestiary of Christ,* trans. D. M. Dooling (New York: Viking Penguin, 1991), pp. 120–21.

3. Marjorie Kinnan Rawlings, *The Yearling* (New York: Collier Macmillan Publishers, 1988), p. 426.

4. Frank Waters, *The Man Who Killed the Deer* (Athens, OH: Swallow Press/Ohio University Press, 1970), pp. 24–25.

Chapter 5 THE JOURNEY BETWEEN LIFE AND DEATH

1. Louise Bäckman and Åke Hultkrantz, eds. *Saami Pre-Christian Religion: Studies on the Oldest Traces of Religion Among the Saamis,* In *Stockholm Studies in Comparative Religion* 25 (Stockholm: Almquist and Wiksell International, 1985), p. 186.

2. T. S. Eliot, *The Waste Land, and Other Poems* (New York: Harcourt, Brace, 1934).

3 and 4. For information on reindeer and caribou, see John Reader, *Man on Earth* (New York: Harper and Row, 1988), pp. 100–106; and David Peterson, *Racks: The Natural History of Antlers and the Animals That Wear Them* (Santa Barbara, CA: Capra Press, 1991).

5. "House of the Reindeer," as retold by Lawrence Millman, *Shaman's Drum* (Midwinter 1989).

6. Rainer Maria Rilke, *Letters (1910–1926),* trans. Jane Bannard Greene and M. D. Herter Norton (New York: W. W. Norton, 1969), p. 373.

7. Mary Elizabeth Williams, "How the Old Woman Met Death," unpublished.

Chapter 6 ANTLERS

1. Rainer Maria Rilke, *Letters to a Young Poet,* trans. M. D. Herter Norton (New York: W. W. Norton, 1963), pp. 29–30.

2. For books describing antler growth, see David Peterson, *Racks: The Natural History of Antlers and the Animals That Wear Them* (Santa Barbara, CA: Capra Press, 1991).

3. Chogyam Trungpa, *Shambhala: The Sacred Path of the Warrior* (Boston: Shambhala Publications, 1988), p. 49.

Chapter 7 THE REINDEER GODDESS

1. Louise Bäckman and Åke Hultkrantz, eds., *Saami Pre-Christian Religion: Studies on the Oldest Traces of Religion Among the Saamis* (Stockholm: Almquist and Wiksell International, 1985), pp. 24ff.

2. Marija Gimbutas, *The Language of the Goddess* (San Francisco: Harper & Row, 1989), pp. 113ff.

3. Bäckman and Hultkrantz, *Saami Pre-Christian Religion,* p. 186.

4. Mary B. Kelly, "Eastern European Embroideries," in *Goddesses and Their Offspring: 19th and 20th Century Eastern European Embroideries* (Binghamton, NY: Roberson, 1986), pp. 33–34.

5. Tore Ahlback, ed., *Saami Religion* (Stockholm: Almquist and Wiksell International, 1987), pp. 27ff.

6. Buffie Johnson, *Lady of the Beasts* (San Francisco: Harper & Row, 1988), pp. 215ff.

7. See Jean Markale, *Women of the Celts,* trans. A. Mygind, C. Hauch, and P. Henry (London: Gordon Cremonesi, 1975), pp. 103ff; and Gimbutas, *The Language of the Goddess,* pp. 113ff.

8. Bäckman and Hultkrantz, *Saami Pre-Christian Religion,* pp. 180ff.

9. See Markale, *Women of the Celts,* and Gimbutas, *The Language of the Goddess.*

10. Mary Elizabeth Williams, "The Fan Maker," unpublished.

11. Modern artworks of antlered deer from dreams or waking visions include those by Alicia Austin, Lori Preusch, Carol Grigg, Elizabeth Golz Rush, Grizella Holderness, Elaine Stanton, Susan Aaron-Taylor, Judith Yahna, and A. V. Pike.

12. Johnson, *Lady of the Beasts,* pp. 215ff.

13. Gloria Feman Orenstein, *The Reflowering of the Goddess* (New York: Pergamon Press, 1990), pp. 88–90.

14. See Suzanne Lovell's video, *Symbolic Healing: A Personal Story* (1990).

Chapter 8 THE WOUNDED DEER

1. See James Balog, *Wildlife Requiem* (NY: Int'l Center of Photography, 1984). Balog shows the way irresponsible hunters abuse deer in his striking photographs.

2. "The Girl and the Evil Spirit," see Marie Louise Von Franz, *Interpretation of Fairytales* (Zürich: Spring Publications, 1973), pp. 131–34.

3. "The Girl and the Moon Man," in *The Sun Maiden and the Crescent Moon: Siberian Folk Tales,* ed. and trans. James Riordan (New York: Interlink Books, 1991), pp. 94–97.

4. See Hayden Herrera, *Frida Kahlo: The Paintings* (NY: Harper-

Collins, 1991), pp. 188–191, and Sarah M. Lowe, *Frida Kahlo* (NY: Universe Publishing: 1991), p. 102.

5. "Mergen and His Friends," in *The Sun Maiden and the Crescent Moon,* pp. 98–101.

6. Euripides, *Iphigenia at Aulis,* trans. Moses Hadas and John McLean, in *Ten Plays by Euripides* (New York: Bantam Books, 1981), pp. 315ff.

Chapter 9 DOE WISDOM

1. "The Enchanted Deer," *The Lilac Fairy Book,* ed. Andrew Lang (New York: Dover Publications, 1968), pp. 151–61.

2. Karl Kopp, "Deer," in *Yarbrough Mountain* (Phoenix, AZ: Baleen Press, 1977), p. 6.

3. Etty Hillesum, *An Interrupted Life: The Diaries of Etty Hillesum, 1941–1943,* ed. J. G. Gaarlandt (New York: Washington Square Press, 1985), pp. 149, 151.

4. Ibid., p. 255.

Chapter 10 THE PATHFINDER

1. Mircea Eliade, *Shamanism: Archaic Techniques of Ecstasy,* trans. Willard R. Trask (Princeton, NJ: Princeton University Press, 1972), p. 8.

2. See Joan Halifax, *Shaman: The Wounded Healer* (New York: Crossroad Publishing, 1982).

3. V. Dioszegi and M. Hoppal, eds., *Shamanism in Siberia,* trans. S. Simon (Budapest: Akademici Kiado, 1978), pp. 303, 388–89.

4. Alexander S. Milovsky, "Tubiakou's Spirit Flight," *Natural History* (July 1992), pp. 35–41. In the Nganasans' legends, Earth Mother and Ice Mother (who personified the cold, nether world) were one until Sun Mother came so close to them that her heat rays separated them and created two auxiliary spirits, Water Mother and God's Mother. Other ancillary divinities were created by God's Mother, who is envisioned as the great reclining naked woman of the middle world, her legs spread wide and water flowing from her vagina into three streams of life.

5. Michael Harner, *The Way of the Shaman* (New York: Bantam Books, 1982), pp. 73–88.

6. For example, the poem, "Snowstorm," by Sami poet Paulus Utsi, tr. Jean Pearson. *Shaman's Drum* (Winter 1987–88).

7. See Ailo Gaup's beautiful novel *In Search of the Drum,* which portrays a contemporary Norwegian Sami's struggle to retrieve the ancient wisdom of his culture (Fort Yates, ND: Muse Publications, 1992); trans. Bente Kjos Sjordal.

Chapter 11   THE REINDEER PEOPLE

1. William W. Fitzhugh and Aron Crowell, *Crossroads of Continents: Cultures of Siberia and Alaska* (Washington, DC: Smithsonian Institution Press, 1988), pp. 244ff.

2. Howard Norman, ed., *Northern Tales: Traditional Stories of Eskimo and Indian Peoples* (New York: Pantheon Books, 1990), pp. 53–55. The Even people are known also as "Lamut."

3. Fitzhugh and Crowell, *Crossroads,* p. 173.

4. Ibid., pp. 212–13.

5. Norman, ed., *Northern Tales,* pp. 261–63.

6. Ibid., pp. 144–45.

7. David Suzuki and Peter Knudtson, *Wisdom of the Elders: Honoring Sacred Native Visions of Nature* (New York: Bantam Books, 1992), pp. 97ff.

Chapter 12   TIME AND HOME ON THE TUNDRA

1. David Suzuki and Peter Knudtson, *Wisdom of the Elders: Honoring Sacred Native Visions of Nature* (New York: Bantam Books, 1992), pp. 181–83.

2. John David Morley, "People of the Eight Seasons," *Destination Discovery* (Dec. 1992), p. 23.

3. James Riordan, ed. and trans., *The Sun Maiden and the Crescent Moon: Siberian Folk Tales* (New York: Interlink Books, 1991), pp. 6–7.

Chapter 13   ARCTIC VISION

1. Rainer Maria Rilke, *Duino Elegies,* trans. J. B. Leishman and Stephen Spender (New York: W. W. Norton, 1963), p. 21.

2. Rainer Maria Rilke, *Letters to a Young Poet,* trans. M. D. Herter Norton (New York: W. W. Norton, 1963), pp. 67–68.

Personal Acknowledgments

My gratitude to the many people who helped me through the struggles of writing this book goes very deep.

First, to Keith Chapman, M.D., my soul mate and companion, who shared the dream of the Reindeer Woman with me; with whom I traveled to the Arctic to see the reindeer and meet the people who follow them; and whose loyalty and love helped me through the varying struggles during my ten-year exploration of the Reindeer Spirit through constant creative dialogue.

I feel inestimably grateful to my women's writing group—Deborah Bowman, Ph.D., and Betty Cannon, Ph.D.—who loved and supported me through a serious writer's block and through so many other difficult obstacles that blocked the way to birthing this book. They were this book's midwives, always present to read the manuscript's many different drafts and to offer their suggestions. Through their playfulness and feminine joie de vivre, they helped restore my sense of humor while I was facing the emotional avalanches and predators that seemed to threaten me and the Reindeer Spirit.

Without the help of Yuri Osipov, Galina Bukova, our Russian interpreter, and Illya and Ivan, our guides, the trip to Siberia would have been impossible. In this respect, my greatest thanks go also to my longtime friend Betty Meador, Ph.D., who in synchronous fashion helped me find the scientist, Yuri Osipov, who made the arrangements to meet the Even people and to participate in the 1992 International Conference on Siberian Shamanism in Yakutsk. Betty Meador also read my manuscript in detail, offering valuable insights and suggestions.

Meeting Michael Hannigan, Ph.D., of the University of Alaska in Nome by "chance" was a unique gift. Michael took us hiking all over the Seward Peninsula and helped us locate caribou and reindeer there.

I owe so much to the help of Marjorie Foster, one of my oldest and dearest friends, an ardent reader whose literary appraisal has always been invaluable. She read the manuscripts of all my books in their nascent form. Marjorie's direct honesty coupled with love always helps keep me on the track of integrity.

So many thanks are due to my writer friends: Lorraine Kreahling, Judy Askew, Cathleen Roundtree, and Karen Chamberlin, who gave me invaluable tips about writing; and to Bill Kittredge, who pointed me along new writing paths during a creative writing conference in the Rockies just as I was starting this book.

I feel very fortunate to have so many talented and caring friends and colleagues helping me with this book in various ways: Lara Newton, Don Williams, Suzanne Short, Kirstin Rasmussen, Ursula Ulmer, Winona Hubrecht, Peer Hultberg, Christina Groff, Don and Barbara Johnson, Ken Ring, Maurice Friedman, Karen Signell, Deanne Newman, Elaine Stanton, Pat Bixby, Lynne Foote, Phyllis Kenevan, Ellen Fox, Sandra Lewis, Karen Kaho, Reed Lindbergh, Harold Booth, Marilyn Corrigan, Karl and Jane Kopp, Myra Shapiro, Jonathon Young, Charlie Abbott, Norma Churchill, Gloria Gregg, and Rennick Stevenson gave me their suggestions as they read various versions of the manuscript and/or discussed ideas with me.

So much inspiration came from my hiking and cross-country skiing friends: Janine Vernon, Sally Klemm, Elaine Stanton, Puja and Utgar Parsons, Deborah Bowman, Steve and Sheri Hunter, Lynne Foote, Steve Wong, Mary Schlessinger, Saul and Phyllis Lowitt, Lynn Leight, Leslie Black and Vance Lemley, Martha Meagher, and Kathy Crumm talked with me about the book while struggling up many mountains. And if I have forgotten anyone who was with me in this process, please forgive me and the vagaries of my memory.

Don Sandner, M.D., who taught me so much about shamanism and its links with Jung, has always been an inestimable source of inspiration, as have my other Jungian and Existential analysts: Hilde Binswanger, Helmut Barz, Joe and Jane Wheelwright, Medard Boss, and Ludwig LeFebre.

I am also indebted to Don Sandner and Steve Wong for organizing the annual ongoing conference on Jung and shamanism every spring and the input from all of its participants. Pansy Hawkwing and her son, Bo, who taught us about Lakota ways, showed us how to build a sweat lodge, enter it ritually, pray, and give thanks, and they shared their age-old wisdom with us, offered a gift and healing so profound I will never forget.

Thanks also to Tom Crumm and the staff of Magic of Skiing for teaching me Aiki skiing, which helped me learn to center, breathe, be present, and transform my fears into enthusiastic discovery, and to enjoy the challenge of steep and bumpy slopes, regardless of blizzards, whiteouts, and subzero temperatures. While skiing with Marge and Ken Blanchard, I learned how challenges of humanistic communication and different learning styles and phases translate into corporate life; they also encouraged this shy introvert to ask for what she needs.

Leo and Suzi Le Bonn of Mountain Travel helped me learn the finer points of trekking and camping in the windy Patagonian wilderness.

The inspiration I have received over the years from Ruth and Robert Bly and everyone at the Great Mother and New Father Camping Conferences is irreplaceable.

Katherine Thalberg and the staff of Explore Booksellers and Bistro in Aspen have provided me with a comfortable, beautiful, and creative writing and reading "home"—a place where I always feel inspired and for which I feel so thankful. Katherine also guided me to rare books about animals.

Many thanks to Timothy White, editor of *Shaman's Drum,* for his beautiful reindeer drawing that expresses the mystery of the antlered ones, and also for his contribution of *Shaman's Drum* to our culture.

I am indebted to my editor at Bantam Books, Leslie Meredith, for her vision, faith, patience, and editorial discernment during this long project; to her assistant, Brian Tart, for his unfailing help on the numerous details of putting a book together; to Linda Gross for her valuable insights and suggestions in the final stage of editing; to her assistant Samantha Howley; and to my agents, John and Katinka Brockman.

And many, many, many thanks to the people participating in my workshops on the Reindeer Woman, all of whom so generously shared their dreams, experiences, images, poems, artwork, and life wisdom with me; and to all of the workshop organizers who made these events possible. (Names and other identifying facts were changed to protect the identity of all contributors of dreams.)

But my deepest gratitude goes to the Even people in Siberia, who invited us to be with them in the Arctic wilderness; to the Sami people of Lapland; to the Inuit and other caribou peoples of Alaska; to all of the indigenous peoples of the earth for their care and reverence of life—and most of all, to those soulful, antlered animals, *the reindeer,* whose hearts, like ours, beat for creation.

Index

D

E